Black
and
Single

Black and Single

*Meeting
and Choosing
a Partner Who's
Right For You*

Dr. Larry E. Davis

The Noble Press, Inc.   CHICAGO

Printed in the United States of America

Library of Congress Cataloguing-in-Publication Data

Davis, Larry E.
          Black and single : meeting and choosing a partner who's right for you / Larry E. Davis
                    p.   cm.
          Includes bibliographical references.
          ISBN 1-879360-29-2 : $10.95
          1. Afro-American single people. 2. Mate selection—United States. 3. Man-woman relationships—United States. 4. Interpersonal relations. I. Title.
HQ800.4 .U6D38   1993
646.7'7'08996073—dc20   93-21565
                                                   CIP

Noble Press books are available in bulk at discount prices. Single copies are available prepaid direct from the publisher.

          The Noble Press, Inc.
          213 W. Institute Place, Suite 508
          Chicago, Illinois 60610
          (312) 642-1168

I dedicate this book
to my wife Shirley
and my mother Clara:
thank you for loving me.

Contents

Acknowledgments

The writing of this book took approximately three years. During that time I became indebted to scores of individuals who made invaluable contributions.

I want to begin my words of appreciation by giving a special thanks to my dean, Dr. Shanti Khinduka, who is also my colleague and friend. Without his steadfast professional and personal support I would never have had the courage to see this book through to completion. This book would also not have been possible without the superb writing skills and editorial assistance of Robert Joiner. He was of tremendous assistance in turning a rather sober academic manuscript into a book that is both understandable and fun to read.

I am also indebted to members of the secretarial staffs in the Washington University School of Social Work: Cynthia Russell, Vivian Westbrook, and Lisa Mathis, and to those in the African and Afro-American Studies department: Adele Tuchler and Raye Riggins. Ms. Russell was especially helpful, reading each of the chapters numerous times and each time providing valuable insights and suggestions.

Many people over the years encouraged me to write this book, but none more earnestly, nor more persistently, than my friend Reginald Ollie. To him I will always be indebted for his admonishment "Davis, you've got to write the book," for his belief in the need for such a book, and for his belief that I could write it! Others too were also supportive: my brothers, Lamar and LaVonne, Alfreda Brown, Jim McLeod, Jerome Hill, Richard Hughes, Warren Anderson, Denise Lombard, Richard Stacy, Brenda Battle, Ernest Reed, Valerie Russell, Michael Powell, and John Pou, who always provided humor to this project.

I also want to acknowledge the efforts of Dr. Eugene Henderson for his supportive role from the very outset of this project. His early efforts allowed me to free up enough time and energy to get out an initial draft. To Gwen Stewart I am also indebted for her careful reading and editing of many chapters.

Finally, I want to acknowledge the editorial efforts and talents of my agent, Denise Stinson. I also want to commend her for doing a marvelous job of quickly getting this book in the hands of a publisher who believed in it. And a special thanks to David Driver, the owner, and Douglas Seibold, the executive editor, of The Noble Press, for taking such care with this book and for getting it to press with such dispatch.

Introduction

"Why bother writing a book about black romance?"

"Isn't black romance the same as everybody else's?"

"Surely it doesn't make any difference whether you're black or white."

"Life is life and love is love!"

These are but a few of the questions and comments I received from critics, friends, and even some colleagues when I told them I was writing a book about black singles. I was taken aback by some of these remarks—which, by the way, came from both blacks and whites. I was surprised because those who raised questions about my topic did not deny that the dynamics of race in American society are powerful enough to affect every aspect of African-American life, including romance. We know, for example, that race affects family income, dynamics, and structure, as well as marriage and remarriage rates. So it should be no surprise that race also plays a significant role in the courtship processes of black singles.

Yet even before receiving feedback from others, I too had asked myself whether I should write a book on black singles rather than on singles in general. This was a difficult, important decision. I was aware that some of what I wanted to say about black romantic relationships was true for all relationships, but I felt that a book addressing the specific concerns of black singles was sorely needed. I also believed that a book providing insights and assistance to black singles might prove of interest to some single white readers also.

I had wanted to write a book on romantic relationships ever since my days as a doctoral student at the University of Michigan. However, it was not until I took a sabbatical at the University of Hawaii that I had the opportunity to begin this project. My desire to write the book was in part due to the fact that as a student I became fascinated by two particular social-science theories: attraction theory, which attempts to explain why we are attracted to some people and not others; and social exchange theory, which contends that our interpersonal relationships are established and maintained according to their relative "costs" and "benefits." I believe that an understanding of the basic tenets of social exchange theory can be particularly beneficial to black singles, who are keenly sensitive to real and perceived social inequities. My conviction about this became apparent to me while I was a guest on a call-in radio show, on which the topic was romance. The show was in its last few minutes when a caller phoned in and asked what I thought was the secret to maintaining romance. I immediately and automatically said, "Fairness." Fairness is at the very heart of romantic longevity. Of course I recognize that (for example) sex, intimacy, and money are among other important issues. But the extent to which you think you're being treated fairly in your relationship determines whether you sustain your romantic involvement with your partner.

In addition to my own professional (as well as personal) interest in the topic of romance, there were other factors pushing me to write this book. First, judging from the considerable media attention given to black male-female relationships, it is clear that black people (like all people) are struggling to achieve a better understanding of their romantic lives. Second, I invariably found myself disturbed and irritated by the poor quality of romantic advice I saw being offered to blacks. Too often black singles have had to rely on folk wisdom, horoscopes, and the "advice" of gossip columnists. I felt that black singles in particular could benefit from the wealth of research on intimate relationships that has accumulated over the past decade.

Finally, as a professor, clinician, and researcher, I have for many years studied and written about the dynamics that affect interpersonal relationships. Recently I finished co-writing a book that in part dealt with black family dynamics. While writing I realized that little of the scholarly rigor given to understanding the lives of black married couples had been devoted to understanding black singles. So, on completing that book, I was even more committed to writing this one.

It is my hope that those who might initially have questioned the need for this book will see from its contents that the concerns of black singles are sufficiently unique to warrant this effort. Take, for example, the fact that the majority of black people are single (which is not the case for a majority of whites). Because so many blacks are single, issues concerning dating are of considerable concern to them.

In addition, the number of black females in relation to black males is grossly out of balance. There are approximately eight black men for every ten black women. This gender imbalance is likely to worsen as the homicide rate for black men continues to resemble that of the populace in a country at war. Moreover, the fact that there are presently more black men in prison than attending college, along with the fact that black men have been losing economic ground relative to everyone else (including black women) over the past few decades, has significantly reduced the percentage of black men perceived to be suitable romantic candidates.

Furthermore, approximately two of every three black marriages end in divorce, compared to one of every two white marriages. This high incidence of divorce means that many blacks are returning to the romantic marketplace for the second or third time. Moreover, the remarriage rate for blacks is comparatively low (only one of three black females who divorces ever remarries). The bottom line is that black men and women are likely to be in the romantic marketplace more often, for longer periods of time, and facing stiffer competition for romantic partners, than are most white men and women.

Aside from these substantial differences in terms of demographic realities, the interpersonal dynamics of black and white couples are also different. For example, white women tend to have more power at the beginning of their relationships, while black women are likely to achieve more power only after their relationships are established. Why? Because the ratio of men to women is more equal for whites; white women have a wider selection of men from whom to choose. Having more options, therefore, results in white women being able to exert more power in the initial phases of romance.

In contrast, because there are fewer black men than black women, black women have fewer romantic options—and thus initially less power when trying to establish relationships. However, unlike most white women, a black woman has an income, education, and professional status that are more likely to be on a par with those of her potential partners. These personal resources are likely to allow black women to wield more power in their romantic relationships in the long run.

Yet another substantial difference between black and white romantic couples involves areas of potential conflict. Unlike their white counterparts, blacks are less likely to face friction caused by romantic partners who refuse to share their resources. Instead, the potential conflict for black couples is more likely to stem from being involved with someone who has few resources to share in the first place. Other issues such as skin color and interracial dating tend to be of greater concern to blacks than whites.

Finally, there is what may be the greatest difference faced by white and black couples: black people must struggle not to perceive their partners in terms of racial stereotypes. More so than white couples, blacks must avoid perceiving their partners in the negative and unfair light in which they are so often portrayed by the media, especially by television and Hollywood. A colleague of mine who teaches political science once joked that he believed that newspapers ran only two types of pictures of black men: those holding some type of ball and those "holding up" somebody. While a clear exaggeration, my colleague's comment captured a sentiment felt by many blacks.

Rarely do we see black romantic intimacy portrayed on television or at the movies, for example. Black women are seldom shown being caressed or kissed; if they are, they are most often shown kissing their friends, children, or parents rather than black men. Think for a moment. In how many movies have you seen Whoopi Goldberg or Oprah Winfrey romantically kiss someone? Usually, when I see black intimacy on the screen, I am struck by its visual novelty—as perhaps you were by the love scenes in Spike Lee's movies *She's Gotta Have It* and *Mo' Better Blues*. These are exceptions to the rule, and take nothing away from my view that, as they attempt to negotiate their romantic relationships, black singles must continually resist seeing each other in negative terms, as individuals who care neither for other black people nor for their own partners and families.

Neither these nor the other differences in the romantic realities faced by blacks and whites mean that black singles and white singles do not share a great many similarities—they do. Nevertheless, these differences necessitate distinct black-white considerations about finding and sustaining romantic relationships.

No one has the power to change the often unpleasant reality confronting you as a black single. I cannot alter the low number of eligible black males in relation to black females, for example. But I can offer you advice to increase your probability of being among those who do have romantic partners. If you take the time to read this book carefully, remember even a few of its basic principles, and apply just a couple of its many suggestions, you will substantially increase your probabilities of finding and sustaining romance—despite what at times must appear to be insurmountable odds.

"Probabilities" is the key word here. My foremost goal is to increase your chances of obtaining greater romantic satisfaction. Your chances of finding romance can be greatly enhanced first by having a better understanding of why you like and are liked by others, and second by recognizing and appreciating those things that make you want to enter and stay in romantic relationships. It is reasonable to assume that a greater understanding of the dynamics of romance will enhance your probability of finding and sustaining romantic happiness. At the same time, no one ever acquires sufficient mastery of romantic relationships so as to be successful every time—no one wins them all! It's important to accept this fact early on. Sometimes you will be successful in getting a certain person to like you, and other times you won't be. Accepting this is important, because it should decrease the amount of time you spend in pursuit of those people who may never really respond to you. Also, recognizing this fact early increases the probability that you will spend more time on those persons who do have sufficient interest in you. The pain and frustration of chasing someone not at all interested in you is an unhappy experience we all have shared. Such apparent losses are inevitable, because some people you might like to know better simply do not value those personal attributes you have to offer.

It was not one of my primary goals to provide information that would "fix" preexisting problematic relationships. In fact, I address only slightly ways to salvage a troubled romance. Instead this book is designed to help you meet and choose new romantic partners. However, in no way do I wish to suggest that beginning a relationship is more important than sustaining one. I elected to focus on the beginning phase of relationships because many people have tremendous difficulty getting romances started. Also, getting off to a good start is so very important to sustaining a successful long-term romantic relationship.

When I appear on talk shows or lecture panels, people often ask me if I have ever experienced difficulties with my own romantic relationships. My answer is "Of course!" I, too, have been a black single, and have been married, divorced, and now recently remarried. Like everyone else, I have struggled with my romantic life. When I acknowledge this fact to audiences, I am often greeted with another question: "If you presumably know so much about romance, then why have you also experienced romantic ups and downs?" I respond to this humbling question in the following way: in some respects understanding romantic relationships is a little bit like understanding electricity. Being knowledgeable about electricity does not exempt me from its effects. In the same way, regardless of the extent of my knowledge, I am subject to the erratic power of romance and its currents.

Having a better understanding of romance should reduce our probabilities of experiencing repeatedly the same type and number of romantic difficulties. More specifically, an enhanced understanding of the dynamics of dating should increase your ability to obtain greater romantic happiness. Yet romance will probably never be so completely under your control as to not require your ongoing attention.

This book draws on the experience of clients, students, colleagues, and friends, as well as upon the research of dozens of social scientists. While writing it I have been conducting research on the dating behavior of black college students. I have spent many hours with black students discussing their concerns about romance. My conversations with these young people were invaluable. To my surprise, the romantic concerns expressed by young black singles are quite similar to those of older black singles. The case studies I have employed involve both individuals and couples, some of whom I have known for many years. They willingly shared their romantic experiences—the good, the bad, and the ugly—with the proviso that I not use their full names. For their time and frankness, I am grateful.

This book covers considerable ground. In Chapter One, I review the major theories regarding mate selection. You may find that your conception of the ideal romantic partner is causing you to select a certain type of person even when that's not the type you really want. You may also discover that you have been relying too heavily on one single romantic criterion in making your selections.

Some will find my bare-knuckles discussion of the mechanics of the dating scene in Chapter Two disturbing. Actually, however, coming to grips with the realities of the romantic marketplace is a must if you are to improve your romantic probabilities. In this chapter, I rely heavily on an expression that is the key to this entire book: *Romantic Market Value* (RMV). It refers to all of those different factors that make you sought-after as a romantic partner. I explain why you must accurately assess your own RMV and how you can best determine your most suitable romantic partners. I also explain why your best romantic strategy is to date partners of equal RMV. In Chapter Three, I suggest ways to determine the most eligible romantic partners for you. In Chapter Four, I briefly consider the importance of color and beauty, both of which black singles continue to be a little nervous talking about, and which continue to exert influence on black romantic relationships.

Chapters Five, Six, and Seven consist of discussions regarding how position and timing affect your romantic opportunities and outcomes. I point out that you must find the place where romance is most likely to happen and then learn how to put yourself in its way. I illustrate the benefits of knowing what "time" it is for you romantically. In this discussion, I offer a variety of tips and suggestions on how you should use time to your advantage in courtship. Finally, I briefly consider some effects that already having had children, or being over thirty years old, may have on your romantic relationships.

Having a clear understanding of the issues I treat in Chapter Eight is, I believe, crucial to sustaining romance. This chapter addresses the issues of fairness and happiness in relationships. Unquestionably, remaining happy in your romance is a chief goal. And perceiving that your relationship is fair is the key to sustaining your happiness. I offer insights into why you may cease to be happy with your partner and why you may remain in a relationship even when you perceive it to be unfair. Power, discussed in Chapter Nine, is often of little concern to those who have it and of considerable concern to those who don't. This, I believe, is borne out in romantic relationships. I review what are likely to be the sources of your power in romantic relationships; you may find that you have more power at your disposal than you think. You may also discover that you could stand to increase the source of your power in some areas. I suggest how you might exercise your power in ways more likely to sustain—rather than undermine—your romantic involvement.

In Chapter Ten, I suggest that your attitude is what's most important. I am in complete agreement with the adage that you often create your own luck. And I encourage you to increase your romantic luck by creating positive, self-fulfilling prophecies. Chapter Eleven offers a variety of strategies for use when you are between romantic partners— a period I call "down time." However brief or long these periods may be, you will soon find out that down time ain't necessarily bad time.

In Chapter Twelve, I offer suggestions for determining whether you are in love, in like, or merely in lust. I also present insights into the distinctions made among the various types of romantic attraction. Chapter Thirteen offers information about the different meanings sex might have for you and your partner. In addition, I discuss how the timing of sex—that is, engaging in it earlier or later in the courtship—may affect the success or failure of your relationship. You may find that your timetable for sex is affecting the type of people with whom you engage in sex. I conclude this part of the book by suggesting how you might enter into a discussion about sexually-transmitted diseases (particularly AIDS) with your partner. I also offer specific steps you should take to avoid contracting such diseases. While this may sound a little unromantic, this is the reality of the 1990s. A fourth of all AIDS victims are black, and black females make up half of all females with AIDS. While I realize that this information can be found via other sources, some black singles (especially young ones) might not take the time to read about the possible perils of sex elsewhere. It is my hope, however, that anyone who is sexually active might take the time to read this information here.

In Chapter Fourteen, I address that always heated topic—dating white. Selecting whites as romantic partners is a topic that invariably raises eyebrows, temperatures, and voices. Foremost in my discussion here, I attempt to bring some insight into the "who and why" of black-white romance. I hope I offer some perspective on its meaning for most black singles. Finally, I conclude this book with a review of some general romantic strategies it would be wise to keep in mind during your romantic pursuits.

If you are serious about improving your romantic life, this book is for you, but be prepared to provide honest answers to some difficult questions along the way. I offer information that will help you create a more satisfactory romantic life, but this is not a romantic "cookbook." As you read, be ready to think critically about your present and past relationships. As the saying goes, "Those who do not know history are doomed to repeat it," and this is as true of romance as it is of everything else. Thus, knowing why things tend to happen as they do allows you to apply what you know to your current situations, even though on the surface your present romantic problem may not resemble those from your past. With this in mind, I offer not only examples of various romantic situations but also the possible explanations that may underlie them. I firmly believe that you will more often know what steps to take in your romantic life if you have a better handle on what causes things to happen or not happen as they do.

Unlike some books on romance, this book does not assume that you are in some way defective; that is, I do not assume that you are suffering from a childhood trauma, experiencing problems of low self-esteem, or are in some way self-destructive. Instead I assume that you are less in need of therapy and more in need of some basic insights into how and why romantic relationships often work as they do.

I have also tried to make the book enjoyable and fun to read. I hope that, in addition to having a few chuckles during the course of reading it, you will also remember some of the practical suggestions it offers. I hope any insights you obtain will remain fresh in your mind, and useful in your present and future romantic encounters.

1 Why You Date Who You Do

I'LL NEVER FORGET those thank-God-it's-Friday parties and the late-night games of bid whist I put together during my graduate-school days. Nor will I fail to remember Suzie, a pleasant-looking sister built close to the ground. She brought much fun to these affairs, partly because of her animated routine whenever she was winning. She'd throw down a trump card hard enough to make the joker frown, then burst into a song. But there was something else that struck me about Suzie: the men she dated. She always seemed to be with someone who, at least on the basis of appearance, appeared to be incompatible with her. One particular evening, I watched Suzie make her usual boisterous entrance on the arm of a new date, this one another grad student named Max. A towering brother with a powerful athletic build, Max looked like he'd just stepped out of the Lakers' lineup. Suzie's head seemed barely to reach his elbow.

This isn't to ridicule Suzie—that would be unwise, because she always had a stinging comeback whenever she sensed she was being put down—or to make light of her romantic choices. After all, she and the men I saw her with always seemed to be fun-loving and happy with the romantic choice they had made. Rather, I mention her because her case demonstrates just how fascinating the psychology of mate selection can be.

On the surface, Suzie's choice of partners seemed outlandish, but she insisted there was a method to her madness. She wasn't in the least embarrassed by what others thought. I followed her into the kitchen that one evening when she went in to refrigerate a bowl of dip that she'd brought. I couldn't help bringing up the subject of mate selection.

"I know what you're implying," she said, feigning irritation. "I read what your friends were thinking as soon as I walked in the door. They looked a little puzzled. But you conservative, educated types always look a little puzzled. I don't take time to try to figure out your hang-ups. Maybe the men I choose don't meet your requirements or expectations. Or maybe you're jealous." She smiled, popped open a beer, then added, "Seriously, I choose my men the way I choose my clothing. I wear what feels right, which isn't the same as wearing what's in vogue."

I knew this was the truth—Suzie was notorious for once having worn a pink running suit to a dinner party.

"And I pulled it off, too, didn't I?" she said, when I reminded her of that night. "But back to the point—believe me, if Max had worn tennis shoes and a tuxedo tonight, I wouldn't have cared because we're so compatible in so many other ways."

Then, in an aside, as her eyes looked out from the kitchen and roamed the crowd in my den, she added, "I can't say the same for some of them folks out there. Most of them look more like brothers and sisters than lovers."

As I said, Suzie insisted there was a method to her madness, but even after all these years I have yet to figure it out. Nevertheless, we all know couples like Suzie and Max, couples who seem oddly matched. At parties, they stand out like two stray socks, incompatible, it seems, in every respect. We also know couples like the ones Suzie mentioned, people who literally resemble brothers and sisters. These two types are only a few of the wide range of mix-ups and match-ups that we can observe in black social circles. If asked for explanations about their choices, many partners would be hard-pressed to offer plausible ones. Getting a handle on our selection processes requires that we look closely at those partners we have chosen in the past. Only then can we fully comprehend how we go about the business of choosing romantic partners. Understanding that process is an important first step toward improving your probabilities of finding and sustaining romance.

If you've never taken a course in the psychology of close relationships, don't feel deprived; few singles in search of partners have. However, what we will do here is review a few of the most common explanations of why people select each other as romantic partners. What we cover will help you comprehend more fully your own situation, and the conscious and perhaps even subconscious processes involved in choosing partners. Without a doubt, applying this understanding to your own circumstances will improve your romantic life.

That's only half the fun, however. My review of the various explanations offered regarding the romantic-selection process will help answer some of your most common questions about your own love life: Why are you attracted to certain types of men or women and not others? Should you date those who are similar to or unlike yourself?

As you read about the following theories of romance, ask yourself how they apply to your selection processes. No single explanation is likely to define in its entirety your own basis for romantic selection. Instead, you will probably find that parts of each of these explanations hold important clues to explaining your prior choices.

Dating Those Who Look Alike

Let's begin with the experiences of Jane, Donald, and Juanita. They are not romantically linked, but they typify the habit of thousands of black men and women who choose the same kinds of mates over and over, some of whom do and some of whom don't satisfy their basic needs. Nonetheless, Jane, Donald, and Juanita continue to gravitate to these types and learn only belatedly, if they learn at all, why.

"Whether I live in Anchorage or Atlanta, I've come to realize that the men I date would look pretty much the same," said Jane, a day care worker. "I've come to that conclusion in recent years, yet I find no rational explanation why it is so. I look back on old photos of guys I've been intimate with and always come away with a sense of wonder. I always ask myself, why am I attracted to men who all look alike?"

Donald, a former president of a national black bank, asked the same question as Jane. "It's not that I have problems finding partners," he said. "It's just that I seem to make as many bad selections as good ones. I guess the biggest surprise came when a close friend told me that if all of my former girlfriends were placed in a room, most people would think they were all members of the same family. Know something? He was right. Why have I been so consistent there?"

Before answering that question, let's quickly review the case of Juanita, an award-winning math teacher, who is as obsessed with numbers in her romantic life as she is in the classroom. She's only five-foot-five, but she's "turned off" by men of average height. More specifically, she never dates any man—no matter how attractive, how eligible, or how compatible—unless he's six-three or taller. "If all my former dates showed up at the same party," she said jokingly, "it would look like a meeting of a professional basketball team."

Joking aside, Juanita is as confused about her selection of romantic partners as are Donald and Jane. What none of these three appear to be aware of is that they are basing their selections principally on looks. Each has a mental image of how a romantic partner is supposed to look; subsequently, each consistently dates people who fit that image. In short, they all have allowed preconceptions, either consciously or subconsciously, to dictate their mate choices. Of course there's absolutely nothing wrong with the mate-hunting approach taken by these three, so long as the chosen partner is also compatible in ways beyond physical appearance. If not, they're often setting themselves up for disappointments—which brings us back to Jane. Instead of asking why every potential partner fits her preconceived notions of what a partner should look like, Jane should also ask herself a more basic question with each new romantic encounter—does a potential partner fit her needs and desires beyond his surface appearance?

Why Jane, Donald, and Juanita all find themselves in the same boat, however, is not as baffling as it might seem. As the psychoanalyst Carl Jung pointed out, each of us has an unconscious representation of what our romantic ideal looks like. He suggests that when Jane (or Donald or Juanita) sees a potential romantic partner who matches her unconscious representation of her romantic ideal, she experiences an immediate attraction toward that person. This rationale can also be used to explain why we may have feelings of "love at first sight."

Whether the foregoing explanation is the actual reason for the similarity in the physical appearances of the mate choices of Jane, Donald, and Juanita, the notion of a mental image of an ideal type does appear to have some validity. Indeed, *many* people commonly select romantic partners who look quite similar to each other. Whether we are aware of it or not, many of us do have some image of how we feel our partners should look. Being aware of that fact helps us understand a lot about why we end up dating certain people and not others—and, perhaps, why we are all the more happy or sad for the choices we made. You may, however, want to resist your typical romantic modus operandi if it appears to be limiting the number of partners who might be good for you. In short, by using looks as your primary or sole criteria in mate selection choices, you are likely to date a number of partners who *look* good to you but who will probably not *be* good for you.

Don't Overlook The Prospects Nearest To You

Just as common as dating clones of our previous partners is the tendency to find potential romance with the girl or guy next door. That hadn't been James's intent when, out jogging in his neighborhood one morning, he all but shouted, "Thank you, Lord!" What he'd found was an appealing woman who lived only three blocks from him—which was another three blocks from Janet, his former girlfriend, and also very close by the woman he'd dated before her. So caught up in his romantic possibilities, James never stopped to ask himself a simple question. Isn't it an enormous coincidence that he has found so many romantic partners so close to home? Is Cupid putting something in the water in this neighborhood, or what? Not until some weeks later did it occur to James that he always seems to date women who live near him, or work in or near the building where he is employed as a draftsman.

Do you consistently date the guy or girl who lives across the hall, across the street, or just a block away? Even if you haven't yet, chances are that you will eventually be attracted to someone close to home— someone who lives, works, or plays near you. This should come as no surprise, since you have the greatest probability of getting to know those people you see most frequently. They are the ones offering you the most convenient ways of getting a romance started. You might strike up a conversation and invite them over for coffee—and hope to be invited in return—just to see how similar or different your homes or lifestyles are. Or maybe you'll find an excuse to drop into their office and exchange a few friendly words. The point is that those with whom you have the greatest probabilities of making contact are also those with whom you have the greatest probabilities of falling in love, or at least getting to know and like.

While living or working close to potential dating partners enhances your probabilities of finding romance, as we shall see, there are some potential disadvantages to this natural tendency as well. Be fore-warned, first of all, that certain work environments are not conducive to romantic encounters. Yours may be one of these if you're in the same boat as Mary. Mary holds a master's degree in library science and recently took a job as chief librarian at a high-powered law firm that employs over a hundred attorneys.

"When the office manager called to tell me I got the job, I was particularly pleased," Mary began, clearly excited. "I saw this job as both a career opportunity and a way to meet eligible men." She paused, grinned wryly and her expression changed.

"My hopes of finding Mr. Right faded real quick. It didn't take me long to discover that, although I head the library department, I was the only black in sight. In fact, I am one of the few blacks in the entire law firm. I'd see a studious-looking black guy stride through my department, but before I got a chance to say much, he'd be gone. The turn-over of the handful of black lawyers here is so high that I never get the chance to establish anything except polite conversation with any of them. Besides, I never get the right opportunity to meet these guys in a less formal setting, like a happy hour, to find out where their heads are."

Mary takes consolation in knowing that her best friend, Imogene, shares the same problem. A secretary, Imogene is fond of blue business suits and silk ties. She fits the corporate image and finds the salary and working conditions pleasant at the headquarters of the Midwestern chemical company where she is employed. Nor, she said, could she ask for more in fringe benefits, except the one she desires most—more professional black men to make her social life as satisfying as her work. Alas, she is the only black in the department. She noted that the company has several black department managers and assistant managers, along with a black vice president—but all are married.

"I made myself *more* miserable socially because I bought a condo in the same suburban community where the firm has its headquarters. I run into only a few single black males, except for a sprinkle of professional athletes, who already have more than their share of company."

Imogene looked as if she'd dug herself an elegant hole and crawled into it. She'd moved from the city into a classy condo nineteen miles away to cut down on the driving time to and from work.

"I've never felt so isolated," she said. "And alone."

"A lot of women would like to be in your shoes," I reminded her. "They'd like to be doing what you do for a living, be able to afford the things your money can buy. And they'd find a way to make positive things happen in their romantic lives.

"Your case isn't all that different from that of a lot of other women. You've cut yourself off from lots of possibilities. I'd sell the condo and move back into the city. Commuting nineteen miles to work everyday may not sound appealing, but you have to weigh that against living in a community where you're more likely to find male company."

As Imogene and I talked over a lunch, a steady stream of buppies and yuppies cruised by. I began to notice how often Imogene seemed to lose track of our conversation as her eyes turned here and there to take in the sight of brothers in BMWs and Corvettes in this section of the city. "This place," she said at one point, throwing open her arms, "is too much. How did I pass it up when I was looking for a place to live?"

The particular men she saw that day might well have been all wrong for her, but there's no denying that Imogene could do wonders for her romantic life by moving back to the city—even into a different, less-expensive neighborhood. In either city location, she's likely to see and meet more than a handful of black males, in a variety of settings. By increasing her encounters with potential romantic partners, Imogene will dramatically enhance her chances of finding and sustaining romance. I'll expand on this subject further in Chapter Five.

The cases of Imogene and Mary also demonstrate one of the more obvious drawbacks encountered by those counting on romantic miracles occurring in their workplaces. They didn't realize that a lot of that sort of success depends on other factors, many of which are within their control. The obvious thing that Mary and Imogene could do— and they could do it with relative ease because they are both young and unattached—is explore other job possibilities that might offer them the important fringe benefit of greater romantic opportunities—that their present jobs lack. Another is to join social and professional orga- nizations where they are more likely to meet eligible men.

The sad fact is that most of the black attorneys that Mary might hook up with never become partners in high-powered law firms. Nor do most black men, with whom Imogene hopes to mingle, find their life's work in the so-called "Big Eight" firms. Many of them have their own firms or are employed by small black-owned businesses. They might not work in office environments that offer intangible amenities, such as breath-taking views of New York's Central Park, or San Fran- cisco's Golden Gate Bridge, or St. Louis's Gateway Arch, but all of this is relative to one's personal priorities. If finding a suitable mate is one of yours, then you might have to move on to less scenic pastures. Clearly, one such pasture is black service-oriented businesses. These businesses are romantically lucrative because they employ and provide services for a number of blacks, with whom you are more likely to come in regular contact. Many of these contacts have the potential of becoming romantic partners.

Allow me to digress a minute to address another aspect of the real world of work. Let's face it: the intermingling between most blacks and whites ends with the work day. They go their separate ways after 5:00, though they may stop together for drinks and happy talk before head- ing in different directions for the night. This superficial intermingling isn't conducive to black romance because blacks in these circles have so few potential partners from which to choose.

Few black women know this feeling better than Rebecca, who used to be the life of these sorts of happy hours, full of witty comments that made her white co-workers feel comfortable as they sipped white Zinfandel. But after happy hour ended on these early Friday eve- nings, Rebecca went with an empty heart to her automobile, drove to her empty apartment, and spent another empty evening alone. That changed, however, after she left the claims-adjustment department of a major insurance firm to take a similar job with a black-owned company. While every male there wasn't a potential husband, Rebecca did find that working for the black company expanded her circle of potential partners outside of the office. Co-workers invited her to parties where she met more people, giving her access to a larger pool of men from whom to choose. While Rebecca is the first to admit that this has yet to lead to a lasting relationship, it has at least given her a shot at some more potential dates. Her attitude now is that her potential romantic partners are likely to be among the men she meets close to her work environment.

While proximity as an explanation for your selection of partners is less intriguing than Jung's notions about our unconscious ideal types, it is, nonetheless, a very good predictor of those you are in fact likely to date. Therefore, those black singles like Imogene who choose to work for firms or live in neighborhoods with low numbers of blacks are actually reducing their probabilities of meeting black romantic partners.

The advantages of finding potential romantic partners close to where we live or work are quite obvious. Less obvious, however, are the potential sources of difficulty. Few couples now know this better than Tom and Sheila. These two had a whirlwind romance before their affections for each other began to fade. But their continued close proximity caused them problems.

Tom, an up-and-coming young executive, lived in a highrise close to his downtown office. He had lived there for about a year before Sheila moved into the apartment across the hall. Like Tom, Sheila was also an aspiring corporate executive and was considered by many to be one of the city's most eligible black women. Tom and Sheila shared many of the same interests and both served on a number of community boards. Right from the beginning, their relationship seemed like a match made in heaven. After some initial courtship they began to date each other exclusively. Yet, after some months, their romance faltered. They became less interested in seeing each other and more interested in seeing others. Meanwhile, they had been spending virtually all of their free time together. Changing things wasn't easy for them. They agreed that in addition to seeing each other, they would begin to date other people.

As you probably can imagine, things immediately got sticky. Living across the hall from each other, they had difficulty not running into each other's dates. This quickly resulted in some awkward moments. Tom and Sheila often saw who visited the other's apartment—and sometimes they were good friends with the new visitors. One early morning, while both were accompanied by their new dates, they all met in the elevator. For the sake of courtesy they had to make what were some rather uncomfortable introductions. Not surprisingly, they soon stopped dating each other all together. Sheila shortly thereafter broke her lease and moved to another apartment building some distance away.

As the experience of Tom and Sheila shows, living or working in close proximity to your romantic partner may rob you of your sense of freedom and independence. However, it is clearly to your advantage to be near a large pool of potential romantic partners. Just remember that not being able to avoid contact with a past romantic partner is likely to make your break-up more painful and difficult.

Dating Those Who See The World As You Do

In spite of the fact that you may be inclined to date a certain "look" or "type," or those people who live or work closest to you, there is no denying that one of the strongest predictors of your attraction to others is their overall similarity to you. Your most pleasant romantic relationships are apt to be with people who share your attitudes, beliefs, and values. This doesn't contradict other factors at work in the selection of your romantic partners, but rather points out the complex process of romance. You are inclined to be most attracted to those who value the same things you do. For example, it is in part because you believe that other blacks hold views and values similar to your own that you are strongly inclined to date them.

There is no doubt that those who share your political views and social agendas are among your best candidates for establishing romance. "Am I black enough for you?" was a common concern in the late 1960s. This expression was not referring to skin color, but rather meant "Am I thinking black enough?" Similarity and attraction tend to be mutual, as those who share your views are also those most likely to like you. Consequently, black social or political functions that are consistent with your values can be good places to find potential romantic partners.

In contrast, you are inclined to find that people who differ from you in their attitudes, beliefs, and values make for unpleasant company. The failure to share similar views with new people we meet actually reduces our desire to meet and speak with those people again. Romantic partners (and friends) who do not share our beliefs about life tend to threaten us by calling into question the correctness of our understanding of situations and events. Most of us in fact avoid establishing relationships with people who do not see things as we do.

Gene and Michelle are good examples of what sometimes happens when opposites attract. He is a Southerner and she a New Englander, but they learned that more than geography separated them. They dated for a month and found themselves arguing constantly during much of that time. "He's a nice guy, but he's too damned cynical," Michelle said of Gene, who's considerably more conservative in his political and social views than she. They found themselves disagreeing heatedly and repeatedly over every social and political issue under the sun, be it school busing or whether a black should run for president. They also quickly found that they were uncomfortable in the presence of each other's friends, because their attitudes, beliefs, and values also differed greatly from their own. Following a big emotional blow-out over the political pros and cons of Jesse Jackson's runs for the presidency, they decided not to see each other any more.

The experience of Gene and Michelle suggests that you probably shouldn't waste time trying to establish a relationship with someone who disagrees with you on too many issues. Nor should you deceive yourself into believing that you can merely "talk away" major philosophical differences, or make your relationship work by changing or compromising your own deeply rooted convictions. Some people who have tried this approach say it only tends to worsen the situation in the long run, because they found themselves questioning whether they could let go of their convictions for the sake of their partner's views. This ambivalence, they report, only led to more arguments and to the prolonging of unsatisfactory relationships that should have ended earlier. The key, then, is to seek partners whose views and values tend to resemble your own. It makes for greater enjoyment and harmony, which, after all, is what you probably want most in a romantic relationship.

Wearing or displaying various symbols such as fraternity pins or letters can help us in this way. Political buttons sometimes serve this purpose too; they tell prospective romantic partners our beliefs about something or someone. If potential partners observe that your beliefs are similar to theirs, they are significantly more inclined to approach you, and let you approach them. It is highly unlikely that you will see a black romantic couple in which one partner is wearing a button supporting Jesse Jackson and the other a button supporting Jesse Helms. However, if you do see such a couple (and they are not in the middle of a big fight), it might be worth your while to ask them how they manage to reconcile their differences.

Those who share our values make us feel confident that we are correct in what we think and do. There is little doubt that having someone who shares a similar outlook may be especially important for you as a black single, inasmuch as you may often find yourself at odds with the views of the white majority. Hence, having a romantic partner who also disagrees with you on almost everything may be too much to bear. Therefore, while it is not necessary to have a partner who agrees with you on everything, it is probably best that you agree on what each of you perceives to be the most important things.

Opposites Attract

Despite the power of similarity, people do sometimes date those who are very different from themselves. I recall being at a dinner party hosted by a couple who run a local black bookstore. Among those at the party were Diane and Bob, who seemed as different as night and day but still appeared to get along fine. After everyone else had left, I stayed behind and listened as the loquacious hostess made random comments to her husband: "Diane," she noted, "is so quiet and Bob is so loud. How can they stand each other? How do they possibly get along? He must drive her crazy. Or is it that she bores him? They will never make it!"

The hostess obviously didn't realize that opposites do sometimes attract. Do your dates seem at times to be the "flipside" of yourself? Couples who are in some ways the opposite of one another may like each other more than those who are in every respect similar. Such couples must somehow complement each other.

With couples who seem to be opposites, partners may have sought out the other to provide them with things they valued but did not themselves possess. Indeed, these "opposite" partners might complement each other in a number of different ways. For example, one partner may have a great need to talk, and the other to listen—as appeared to be the case with Diane and Bob. Or one may have a need to control and the other to be controlled, or one to nurture and the other to be nurtured.

Actually, when most people speak of opposites attracting, they are not generally referring to such things as race, attitudes, values, or beliefs. Instead, when black couples are attracted to others who differ from themselves, it is usually along the lines of some personality trait or behavioral style. Most often, couples who are said to be the "opposite" of each other are not necessarily opposites in terms of being liberal or conservative, saint or sinner, rich or poor.

It probably is also the case that Diane and Bob were initially attracted to each other for the things they shared. Perhaps later they found that being opposites in certain respects made getting along with each other easier. A difference in styles of behavior may be less noticeable to those who are already dating than to those who are just getting started. By contrast, we may be especially sensitive to what we perceive to be our potential romantic candidates' personal styles and hence, presumably, their needs relative to our own, during our *first* meeting with them. Indeed, the expression "They appeared needy" probably most often means that those people needed things that we had no need to give them.

In summary, you may very well be attracted to people who seem different from you. But they are likely to differ from you more in terms of style than substance. In other words, they are still likely to be Baptist if you are, poor if you are, anti-abortion if you are. And yet they may express themselves differently than you do—softly or loudly, aggressively or passively. The dissimilarities between yourself and your partners do sometimes enhance your relationships; those who have personal qualities which you like or need, but do not possess, may make you feel more complete. They may also make your own shortcomings less noticeable. A word of caution, however. Don't get carried away with this idea—even if you are attracted to someone who is the complete opposite of yourself, the odds are against the two of you staying together as a couple. You must, if you are to sustain a romance, be more alike than different regarding those things that are most important to you.

Dating Equals

Are you attracted to people who appear to be equally as attractive, wealthy, or educated as yourself? Do you attempt to seek out romantic candidates whom you feel are "on your level" or who appear to have as much going for themselves as you feel you do? If so, you are engaging in what is known as social exchange. This notion of romance defines getting along with others as a process of give and take. It holds that the best relationships are those people perceive as being fair. You may ask how your perceptions of fairness are relevant to establishing romantic relationships. Let's take a closer look at what appears to be a tit-for-tat notion of romance.

Richard, a lawyer, dates only women whom most men would consider to be very good looking. Maria, a secretary and former beauty queen, is regarded by many men as an absolute knock-out, and she refuses to date anyone who isn't what she calls "a professional." Many people would view both Richard and Maria as being stuck-up buppies. Their attitudes are not unusual, however. They are only examples of what most of us do, whether we elect to acknowledge this process openly or not. Generally, it seems that we do try to date people who are as equally desirable a romantic partner as we are.

To do this, however, you must have some idea of your own romantic desirability, or your romantic market value (RMV)—the value of all of your "assets" (such as beauty, wealth, prestige), minus your "liabilities" (such as little education, unemployment, or lack of social graces). In short, your RMV is all the things you have going for you minus all those things you don't. (Michael Jordan, for instance, can safely be said to have exceptional RMV.) You may date someone who has different qualities than you, or more or less of the same qualities, but for you to experience the sense that you have made a fair romantic deal or found a "good catch," your date's RMV must add up to a total approximately equal to your own.

It is unlikely that a potential romantic partner will have exactly the same romantic strengths and liabilities that you do, so in order to strike what you perceive as a fair deal, you are most often required to engage in a series of exchanges, or trade-offs, of various attributes. The case of Richard, the attorney, and Maria, the secretary, will suffice to illustrate this. Both have high RMVs, though they are the product of different sources. Though not especially handsome, Richard draws his high RMV from his six-figure salary. Maria, by contrast, earns only $15,000 a year. Her high RMV lies foremost in her beauty.

Improved economic and professional status can also change our perceptions of our RMV in relation to others. That certainly explains the change in Lester's attitude once he was promoted to vice-president at the bank where he'd worked for seven years. He felt that the raise that went with his promotion made him a better romantic catch. He was right, judging from the fact that he received more romantic offers than ever before, and was able to be more choosy in selecting partners.

The same was true of Gwen. After she earned her MBA, she became restless about her romantic life, feeling the men she dated no longer seemed to measure up. She began to feel she deserved a mate who had a financial future comparable with her own. Cold as it might seem, Gwen broke off her relationship with her old boyfriend shortly after receiving her advanced degree. Ironically, she now dates a male who is somewhat less handsome but who also has an MBA, and a lot more in common with herself. In short, both Lester and Gwen rightly perceived that their RMVs increased as a consequence of their career advancements.

The case of Gwen demonstrates that relationships tend to sustain themselves only when partners feel they are reaping the romantic rewards they deserve, in relation to what they might be able to obtain from an alternative relationship. People do, of course, sometimes leave relationships even when no alternative relationships are readily available. This situation is perhaps best captured in the expression, "I can do bad by myself." They have, by some means, come to the conclusion that their current level of satisfaction is too low when weighed against the costs required to sustain the relationship. In other words, it appears that an existing relationship, despite the absence of a possible replacement, can become less rewarding than the option of no relationship.

Like Richard and Maria, most of us try to find partners who seem to offer us a good "deal." We have all heard comments from our parents and friends that someone is or is not a good catch, or is or is not in our league. Our allies are forever attempting to see to it that we do not sell ourselves short in the romantic marketplace. The point is that people with romantic-desirability levels equal to your own are the ones who make up your "field of romantic eligibles," the people you are most likely to date. These are the individuals your parents have in mind when they urge you to hang out with "your kind of people." These are perhaps the folks we have in mind when we speak of "together people." We may sometimes refer to those people whom we perceive to have even slightly more going for themselves than we do as being phony, uppity, or "bougie."

No single theory can completely explain why we are drawn to certain people. Each of these romantic theories of attraction probably plays a part in your selection of romantic partners. However, I believe that many of the most useful concepts in understanding dating processes are those outlined in what psychologists refer to as social-exchange theory. And the social-exchange theory of mate selection tells us that falling in love is a very deliberate process. Its basic theme is that before we allow ourselves to get involved with someone, we consciously or unconsciously attempt to determine whether they are our romantic equals. Most people use perceptions of their own level of romantic desirability as criteria in determining the romantic suitability of others, which is why it is important to have an accurate assessment of your own romantic desirability. In this sense, your criteria—your RMV—serve as the gatekeeper to your romantic relationships. This is a concept I will develop in further detail in Chapter Two.

Some of you may feel that the social-exchange ideas of attraction make individuals appear to be shrewd and calculating, if not mercenary. And yet, if you look at the romantic selections made by those around you, it does not appear that your friends and family members are falling in love at random, as your most noble beliefs about romance would suggest. Instead, numerous variables—including race, physical attractiveness, social status, money, education, and religion—clearly affect romantic selection. In this respect, the social-exchange theorists offer the best evidence to support their basic claims. Thus, it's upon this seemingly unromantic theory of romance that my discussions of meeting and choosing partners rely most heavily.

2 Assessing Your Romantic Market Value

I WAS IN A BOOKSTORE one day when I overheard a woman whose voice I recognized talking to another woman she obviously hadn't seen in a long time. The conversation got around to romance. "There must have been twenty good-looking men at that party," she was saying, "but you know me, honey, I pick my men the way some people pick lottery numbers—randomly. And, girl, would you believe I came up with a winner. You gotta meet him . . . "

The woman doing the talking was named Jean. I knew it was her as soon as I saw those unmistakable dimples on her chocolate-brown skin—she happened to be an old classmate of mine. She always sat in the front row, in bleached blue jeans—very attentive, very bright, and always asking a lot of questions. I hadn't seen Jean in quite a while. After asking about the latest on our mutual classmates, I asked how her love life was going. She laughingly answered, "Great." She had heard that I was conducting research and giving workshops on romantic relationships, so I invited her to attend my next workshop. She thought that would be fun, so I gave her the time and she agreed to be there.

I decided that at this next workshop I would test Jean's "love is random" theory. So at the very start of the workshop I asked those attendees who believed that falling in love is a random process to raise their hands. Jean immediately put her hands to her mouth; she realized I'd overheard part of her conversation at the bookstore. She raised her hand. To her surprise most of the others present did too. They had little doubt that love was random—at least until I asked several other questions that dispelled their illusions. How many of them considered religious preference when choosing partners, I asked. A few hands went up. Then I asked how many considered educational level when choosing partners. A few more hands rose. Still more people raised their hands when I asked how many took physical attractiveness into consideration. Finally, I asked how many took race into consideration when selecting partners, and nearly all hands were raised. By then Jean was blushing, perhaps realizing, as did the others in attendance, that there was *nothing* random about how she'd picked her partner. Though most of them conceded as much, many still found it hard to let go of the idea that they were not "biased" in their selections of romantic partners.

Make no mistake about it: black romance is not a random process. You are meticulous in choosing partners—using a variety of factors, ranging from religion to income, as your yardstick—and so is everybody else. In other words, you size up a potential partner in deliberate ways before deciding whether that person might be suitable.

I tune in to a lot of conversations and observe behavior a great deal when I am among black professionals, especially in social settings. "What do you do for a living?" is one question I hear a lot. It is raised in a matter-of-fact way, but the people doing the asking aren't just making idle conversation. They're asking a serious question. In fact, this question is so routine, in almost any social setting where upwardly mobile blacks gather, that some seem to anticipate it by exchanging business cards that attest to their high professional status.

One Friday after work, I was having a drink at just such a gathering with a friend from Detroit. Married and in his late fifties, he said he'd forgotten how competitive mate-hunting could be, and how much things had changed since his single days. He thought that two things in particular had changed. First, he thought women seemed more assertive in their romantic pursuits. For example, he was surprised to see some of the women there approach men and attempt to start conversations with them. Others, he noted, even bought men drinks— something that certainly didn't happen much when he was dating. Second, he thought that men were more discriminating, in that they sought out women who were not only good-looking, but also appeared to have a lot going for themselves professionally, in terms of earning power. In short, he concluded that women in today's dating scene behave more like men than they used to, and men behave more like women.

"These young black professionals are really quick on the draw, aren't they?" he said, watching them with a certain fascination. "The brothers and sisters are handing out business cards with everything on them except their Social Security numbers and incomes. And I'm sure they'd be happy to supply those upon request." He noted, however, that there were advantages to this quick-draw approach. It saves time and, in most instances, it gets the attention of a prospective partner long enough for them to begin a conversation.

The objective of those singles who hand out their cards, as well as those who ask what you do for a living, is often the same. They want to select the most desirable partner available; they're giving out and taking in information in an effort to assess the desirability of those around them. They're serious about finding the best possible deal. To determine what is or is not a good romantic deal, however, you must first have some idea of the value of your own romantic marketability. Most of us think we know our level of romantic marketability, but our assessments are rarely, if ever, fully objective. Because each of us is inclined to hold ourselves in the most favorable of lights, getting an accurate reading of our romantic marketability is often difficult to do.

Assessing Your Value

Perhaps this hard-nosed analysis of relationships sounds cold, calculating, unromantic—it raises unpleasant issues many of us would rather avoid. Jesse Jackson captured the essence of why an analysis of this type is essential, though, when he said, "Reality will tolerate our fantasies but it will not spare us the consequences." In other words, we can pretend that something we do not like does not exist, but our denial of it will not cause it to go away. We may wish to deny that those in the romantic marketplace evaluate our romantic desirability, but the fact is that they do.

Your desirability in this marketplace, or what I elect to call your Romantic Market Value (RMV), is a function of the sum of all of the positive assets and negative liabilities you bring to your relationships. Most of us, however, are often poor at assessing our own RMV. What makes our assessment go awry is our tendency to overestimate our assets and underestimate our liabilities. Our family and friends are often of little assistance, because they typically tell us everything that is "right" about ourselves, discreetly failing to mention our shortcomings; they distort our self-perceptions, exaggerating our virtues and minimizing our faults. I am not suggesting that you *not* use your family and friends as resources, but you should also rely on advice from individuals who may find it easier to be objective. If possible, seek personal appraisals from those outside your circle of family and closest friends. Those closest to you are likely to be the last to tell you that you need to lose weight, get in shape, go back to school, or get your teeth straightened. Also, try to ask for readings on your RMV from members of both sexes, as men and women may evaluate you differently.

Your prior romantic experiences may also serve to inform you of your RMV. For example, experiencing consistent frustration in your attempts to date certain types of people may be your best indication that you are aspiring beyond your romantic reach. Let me remind you that most people are expecting to receive as much as they feel they have to offer in a relationship. So don't anticipate that someone will look past the shortcomings of your RMV and fall for the "the real you." It may happen, but don't count on it—you're most likely setting yourself up for disappointment. Even if you receive initial reactions from people who have substantially higher RMV than yours, the odds are against your sustaining those relationships.

That was the case with Jake, a less-than-handsome computer programmer in his mid-thirties. He could never quite figure out that he not only had to find a mate he liked, but one who also liked him. Unfortunately, he consistently sought out women who were exceptionally attractive, very well educated and considerably more sophisticated than he. These women, he told me, were often nice when he first met them. Some were willing to go out with him for a drink or dinner (usually at his expense), but they always seemed to brush him off when he tried to move things to a more romantic level. Either they failed to return his phone calls, suddenly got back together with old boyfriends, or told him that they just wanted to be friends. Jake was often devastated and depressed following these rejections, but he never seemed to consider that maybe these women were out of his league.

Personal attributes that are observable or easily made known to others are critical to the beginning of a romantic courtship. Your race, physical attractiveness, age, educational level, employment status, and occupation are some of the key factors with which other black singles will be most immediately concerned. These RMV factors can be viewed as the "gatekeepers" of romance, because they are critical in determining who you let into your life and who you keep out. While sharing similar RMVs is no guarantee that couples will stay together, it is the best predictor of who will most likely get together in the first place.

Are RMV factors superficial? Some people may think so. But most of us use this type of information every day. These factors provide the most basic sorts of information about us. They have a profound effect on what we spend much of our time thinking and talking about. Like it or not, our levels of physical appearance, income, educational attainment, and professional status are not unimportant aspects of our lives. Ignoring their importance puts you at great risk of continued romantic disappointment.

Yet it is important to keep in mind that the relative importance of these gatekeepers may vary for certain groups of the people. Artists, for example, or others with less-traditional professional identities, may place greater importance on certain attributes than the rest of us. For example, they may want a partner who is unconventional in appearance and/or lifestyle. But whatever a person's hierarchy of RMV attributes, don't be fooled into thinking that such a hierarchy isn't important. In all but rare instances, having sufficient RMV is the key to your entering someone's romantic life. Most of your potential romantic partners will be inclined to hold off on evaluating your more personal qualities until they first establish whether you have enough "objective" RMV qualities to make you a "worthy" candidate.

I am sure that some of you are thinking about the obvious mismatches in RMV that you have seen. Yes, they do occur—but these are the exceptions. People who are able to attract the romantic attentions of those with significantly greater RMV than themselves have, so to speak, hit the Lotto. They have accomplished an unlikely feat which, in part, is why they stick out in your memory.

The goal of this book, however, is to increase your probabilities of finding and selecting new romantic partners. To accomplish this task you must steer away from tactics that have lower probabilities of successful romantic outcomes, and take up those that have the highest probabilities of success.

Perhaps you are asking, "What about feelings and personal qualities? Don't these count for anything in determining a person's desirability? What about 'me'? I want someone who likes me for *me,* not for my college degree or bank account." These concerns are legitimate. Qualities such as a pleasant personality, kindness, or a good temperament are likely to become more important in the later phases of courtship, however, after prospective partners have first met these other, less-romantic qualifications. None of us wants to fall in love with someone whose primary means of employment turns out to be dealing drugs or prostitution, irrespective of how kind or good-tempered they are. It is for this reason that most initial courtship efforts are directed toward determining if we should allow ourselves to become involved with certain individuals. As a result, we run what amounts to a quality-control check to see if our potential partners meet our basic qualifications. We are then left with the more "romantic" task of deciding if we like them or not! To put it another way, factors such as feelings and personality will weigh heavily into what happens to your romance, but only after your potential partners have first demonstrated that they deserve your attention—or that you deserve theirs.

Much of what will determine whether you are interested in someone can be, and often is, obtained within a very few minutes of your first meeting. In fact, some of this information may be obtained even before you have a chance to interact. For example, many black singles rely heavily upon the use of sorority and fraternity affiliations, or the use of status symbols such as designer clothes and expensive cars, to make statements about themselves. At the very onset of potential romantic encounters, the vast majority of information available about people is visual information. Indeed, many would argue that black singles place too great an emphasis on physical appearance, membership in high-status associations, and material factors in general in their attempts to attract romantic partners. While this is probably true, it is also true of most people in most social groups. Most people tend to match up according to the RMV factors that are most important for their particular groups.

In any case, by the time most of us reach adulthood we have become quite familiar with those factors associated with romantic desirability. We have also received considerable feedback as to our own level of romantic attractiveness. Moreover, we also understand that our RMV is subject to fluctuations. For example, we are acutely aware that the gain or loss of thirty pounds may make a very significant difference in our degree of physical attractiveness to others and, hence, may influence significantly our romantic desirability. Similarly, graduating from student to professional, being promoted, winning the lottery, or inventing a new product for which there is a great demand is a plus to your RMV. In short, any alteration of your life that adds to your overall assets is likely to increase your value in the romantic marketplace. On the other hand, those changes that reduce your assets decrease your value in the romantic marketplace—losing your job, for example.

The blues have always captured so much of what is really going on in life; hence, it is not surprising that a blues song would demonstrate this point so well. For example, B.B. King sings a song that demonstrates how one's RMV can change over night. It seems that after his woman left him, a man went to Las Vegas and won $50,000. As B.B. sings, word about winning $50,000 can "get around and make a lost cause come up found." She later attempted to get back together with him, but he refused. It seems she may have made her move too soon.

Most of us have relatively stable RMVs. In general, we are not subject to rapid or extreme changes in our level of romantic desirability. Barring some unforeseen event, most of our gains or losses in RMV are likely to be only moderate in their effect. In contrast, entertainers and athletes are at great risk of having wide swings in their RMVs. Their careers are subject to extreme highs and lows, and thus, so are their levels of romantic desirability. There is little doubt that these wide fluctuations in the RMVs of black celebrities contribute to their frequent propensity to change romantic partners. Magazines such as *Essence, Jet,* and *Ebony* keep us up to date on the economic and professional status of black superstars. People who experience extreme changes in their economic and professional situations may have a greater tendency to leave or be left by their partners, as their fame and fortunes rise and fall.

Be realistic in assessing your RMV. You must be able to take a good look at what you bring to prospective relationships relative to what others are likely to bring. I am not suggesting that you should settle for less than you deserve in a romantic partner, but rather that you attempt, as accurately as possible, to assess your romantic desirability. Failing to do so may result in your spending too much time in the search, and not enough in the company of those you want very much to be your romantic partners and friends.

I recommend that you make a written list of your romantic assets similar to the one below. This list obviously does not include all of those personal assets you value. Your personal RMV list will, therefore, be longer and more comprehensive. The list here is only intended to capture the most common factors we notice about people, and which they notice about us. A potential romantic partner's assessment of you will not be *completely* determined by these factors, but they will almost always be included in his or her romantic assessment of you.

On the scale below, rate yourself on how you feel you stand on each factor (one being low and ten being high).

Your RMV Assessment Scale

Level of attractiveness   1 2 3 4 5 6 7 8 9 10
(Unattractive) (Average) (Very Attractive)

Employment Status   1 2 3 4 5 6 7 8 9 10
(None) (Part-time) (Full-time)

Professional Status   1 2 3 4 5 6 7 8 9 10
(Unskilled) (Semi-professional) (Professional)

Annual Income   1 2 3 4 5 6 7 8 9 10
(0-$15,000) ($15,000-$30,000) ($40,000 and above)

Education   1 2 3 4 5 6 7 8 9 10
(High School) (College graduate) (Graduate degree)

Social Status   1 2 3 4 5 6 7 8 9 10
(Low) (Medium) (High)
(Among your friends, colleagues, and the broader community)

Other Factors   1 2 3 4 5 6 7 8 9 10

After you have reviewed your own RMV list, complete one for the romantic partner you would like to find:

Your Partner's RMV Assessment Scale

Level of attractiveness   1 2 3 4 5 6 7 8 9 10
        (Unattractive) (Average) (Very Attractive)

Employment Status   1 2 3 4 5 6 7 8 9 10
        (None) (Part-time) (Full-time)

Professional Status   1 2 3 4 5 6 7 8 9 10
     (Unskilled) (Semi-professional) (Professional)

Annual Income   1 2 3 4 5 6 7 8 9 10
   (0-$15,000) ($15,000-$30,000) ($40,000 and above)

Education   1 2 3 4 5 6 7 8 9 10
   (High School) (College graduate) (Graduate degree)

Social Status   1 2 3 4 5 6 7 8 9 10
         (Low) (Medium) (High)
  (Among your friends, colleagues, and the broader community)

Other Factors   1 2 3 4 5 6 7 8 9 10

After reviewing your answers, ask yourself, "Am I using what I would like to obtain from a romantic partner, rather than what I actually bring to a relationship, as the gauge of my own romantic value?" Ask yourself also, "Is my romantic market value equivalent to that of the romantic partner I seek? Am I asking for more than I have to offer?" As the saying goes, there ain't no such thing as a free lunch and nobody rides for free! So, don't expect to get much more than you have to offer. Otherwise you are only setting yourself up for disappointment, if not immediately, then soon. Remember our example of Jake, the computer programmer. Prospective romantic partners may accept temporarily an RMV inequity in what they feel they deserve, but they are typically only holding on to what they have (you) until they can find what they really want. I'll talk more about this dynamic in Chapter Eight.

We generally feel quite strongly that the people we date should have as much going for them as we do. Situations where our dates have either a great deal less or more RMV than we do are prone to cause problems. If, for example, we perceive our partner as having a lower

RMV than we do, we are inclined to feel we should do better. We may feel that we are somehow being cheated, or at least not getting what we deserve from the relationship. On the other hand, if we perceive that our partner's RMV is greater than ours, we're likely to feel insecure. In relationships where partners start out about equal but one somehow achieves a higher RMV than the other—by winning the lottery or somehow becoming a celebrity, for example—the lower-RMV partner may break off the relationship. This may occur because such people sometimes feel unable to "carry their weight" in the dating relationship.

In life, however, merely having a high RMV doesn't necessarily mean you will get selected by the partner you desire. That's because we often miscalculate our value, or it fluctuates; also, our overall "worth" is subject to the "values" important to our would-be romantic partners. For this reason, the "best" black man or woman does not always "win." In many instances, you may feel you have lost out on a relationship to someone who has less going for them than you do.

What you don't always know, and never have control over, are the values held by those persons for whom you are competing. For example, which of the candidates listed below would you prefer to date, if you had to make your decision based only on the information provided? The candidates have been assigned specific values among various attributes. The range runs from one to ten, with one being the lowest and ten the highest.

Compare partners #1 and #2 with partners #3 and #4:

#1		#2	
1. Attractiveness	7	1. Attractiveness	9
2. Profession	6	2. Profession	6
3. Income	$25,000	3. Income	$15,000
#3		#4	
1. Attractiveness	9	1. Attractiveness	5
2. Profession	8	2. Profession	6
3. Income	$30,000	3. Income	$20,000

Predicting the higher RMV of #3 versus #4 is likely to be easier than doing the same for #1 versus #2. We are inclined to say that #3 has a higher romantic market value than #4. In the absence of other information, #3 is the romantic candidate most of us would choose.

On the other hand, deciding between romantic candidates #1 and #2 is tougher because it requires you to make value decisions. Thus, your RMV is influenced not only by your objective attributes, such as profession and income, but also by how important these attributes are to those you want to attract. Your specific preferences are most likely to come into play only when you are forced to make a choice between candidates with different attributes. If, on the other hand, both candidates have the same positive attribute, you are likely to perceive the candidate who has the most of that positive attribute as being the most desirable.

Who Should You Try To Date?

One recent weekend at a college workshop on black male-female relationships, a tall, thirtyish, ebony-hued woman stood up to tell the audience what she desired most in a romantic partner. Her name was Mary Alice, and her desires were downright insatiable. She wanted a man who was exciting and wealthy, handsome and well-educated, progressive in his politics and traditional in his sexual mores. And, yes, he had to take her to a foreign country every year.

I remember thinking that this sister wanted an awful lot in one person, given my initial superficial assessment of her own RMV (an assessment that later turned out to be right on target). Though I was the workshop moderator, I wanted to step out of my role and say, "Be serious, Mary Alice." And the audience apparently agreed with me, judging from the groaning that followed her comments.

Anyway, I got to know Mary Alice a little better during an early evening reception at the college's black cultural center. I was surprised how easily she talked with me, a stranger, about the unrealistic schemes she had concocted over the years to land a suitable partner. She talked, sipping wine and peppering her comments with little humorous put-downs of herself. These she employed, I gathered, in order to make light of her romantic disappointments, and to explain in a roundabout and defensive way how she came to desire so many things in one man.

Although her late father had been a Pullman porter in Chicago, it turned out that he had acquired enough rental property and independent income to expose her and her mother to what Mary Alice regarded as the finer things in life—French restaurants, occasional vacations overseas, and a summer home in Idlewild, a Michigan resort where, as a kid, she'd mingled with upper-middle-class black people she otherwise might not have met. Her mother had insisted that she attend Fisk University, half hoping she'd find a husband who'd provide her with the lifestyle to which she'd become accustomed. The fact that she came to the workshop alone told me she probably hadn't gotten noticed by the "right" man over a decade later.

In situations like hers, I usually grope for a metaphor that might help to bring the person down to earth. The right one came to me later that evening as the reception crowd thinned and some of us, including Mary Alice, watched the final minutes of a boxing match in which Sugar Ray Leonard demolished an opponent. During the count, Mary Alice was so caught up in the excitement that she shouted: "Sugar Ray ought to take on Mike Tyson next." Sugar Ray versus Mike? The brothers surrounding the TV took her comment as a joke, but I realized she wasn't kidding.

Boxing, I believe, is a good metaphor for romantic misadventures. Some of us have been in the ring of romance far too long, taking on all comers and bypassing those with whom we are most evenly matched. To a great extent our romantic success depends on seeking potential romantic partners who are within our own weight class, so to speak. Failure to take this principle to heart will likely result in a poor romantic record.

Finally, *don't cheat on your assessment!* The main point of this entire discussion has been to show how and why couples are, at least initially, likely to match up. Whatever insights you might have obtained from this section will be wasted if you fail to be honest and objective in assessing your RMV and that of those you wish to date. I also believe that you will find it beneficial to acknowledge the fact that your romantic choices are not as random as you were told they are "supposed" to be. Once again, try to get a realistic grasp of your RMV; gross miscalculations will only result in romantic frustration, and ultimately delay your chance to establish a lasting relationship.

Do Couples Always Match Up Evenly?

Do the RMV attributes I have discussed always determine who dates whom? No, despite the fact that a wealth of evidence suggests that people do tend to match up fairly evenly with respect to apparent RMV. There seem to be some instances of both "under" and "over" romantic achievers. However, let me state right away that while both of these situations occur, they do so with considerably less frequency than equal match-ups. It is also true that instances of underachievement are probably more common than overachievement, even though many people like to think of themselves as falling into the overachiever group.

How does romantic underachievement occur? We have all seen instances where the romantic lives of some of our friends and relatives fail to keep pace with their apparent RMV. For some reason, they are rarely able to sustain dating relationships with people who appear to be their romantic equals. Even though they frequently go out with "great dates," they cannot seem to maintain a relationship with any of their prospects. When this occurs, it is likely that their RMV—based on such factors as their level of physical attractiveness, social status, and income—might be greater than their level of personal and social maturity.

Take the case of Paul, a professional basketball player. This young black man from Los Angeles is great on the court, but his social skills are far less developed than his athletic abilities. Away from the game, he turns out to be a frequent embarrassment to his dates. He's got lots of money, but as one of his dates said, "The boy ain't got no style." He's a social Neanderthal. Paul's dates cannot accommodate his lack of social graces, despite the fact that he does possess a number of highly desirable attributes.

Factors such as professional status, income, and physical attractiveness are often better at predicting if we will be allowed to initiate a particular relationship, rather than how well we will do once actually in that relationship. That is, your RMV might determine whether you get an opportunity to "try out" for a romantic position, but it doesn't guarantee that you get to play, as is the case with Paul.

In contrast, some people appear to be romantic overachievers. For example, their level of RMV indicates that they are dating people who are their romantic market superiors. Instances of romantic overachievement are rare, principally because it can be so difficult to get the attention of those who perceive themselves as having a substantially higher level of RMV than we do. However, as we all know, it does happen. Most often relationships in which one partner has an apparent RMV higher than the other are the result of specific situations. For example, a couple might have become romantically involved while working together on some professional or civic project. As a result of their "forced" interaction, the couple might have established a relationship without having gone through the typical "screening" process. In other words, the normal gatekeepers were not in effect, thereby giving the person with the lower RMV an opportunity to approach or be approached by the normally inaccessible higher-RMV person.

One case that comes to my mind is that of Joanna, a female executive who headed the community affairs department for a brewery, and Bob, her male secretary. He happened to be among the very few black office staff members. Romance was far from Joanna's mind when she began having lunch with him, discussing office politics and her unique problems with managing a mostly white staff. She enjoyed Bob's company, partly because he helped her relieve the pressure of the job and didn't feel threatened in the least about having a woman as a boss. Their meetings moved from the brewery's cafeteria to after-work drinks and later to dinners—all of which confirmed Joanna's views that her secretary was warm, charming, and witty, a man secure in his masculinity who didn't feel at all threatened by her. I'll have to disappoint you: Joanna and Bob dated for some time, but eventually married other people.

If their situation shows the potential in dating someone with lower RMV than yourself, it also points up the risks. Joanna's family and friends had a way of reminding her—in subtle and not so subtle ways—that they felt something was amiss about her romance. What they meant was that something was odd about a female executive dating a male secretary. They also felt, without really knowing Bob, that he was merely taking advantage of Joanna.

This kind of suspicion on the part of family members and friends is not unusual. Our friends and relatives are especially sensitive to the perception that we may be making a bad romantic deal. Indeed, it is in part due to this type of social pressure that black women like Joanna have generally resisted suggestions that they date or marry black men who are less educated or less professionally advanced than themselves. This is why Joanna's romance with Bob didn't work out. While Bob never felt uncomfortable in the presence of Joanna's family and friends, he discerned *her* discomfort. He eventually asked for a transfer out of Joanna's department, and out of her life.

Joanna's situation is not unique for black professional women, many of whose circumstances may force them to choose from a small pool of partners who are less socially and professionally accomplished than they are. Their choices can pose innumerable problems, according to Joanna. She enjoys attending events that are not only socially rewarding but culturally stimulating, like the theater, the symphony, and openings at the art museum.

She said, "I didn't feel in the least embarrassed about being accompanied to these social events by Bob, although there were some trying experiences. I'd see people who'd make a point of prying into my business and asking Bob all sorts of personal questions about what he did for a living, and once they found out, they'd quickly move on to talk to someone else, as if a man who was a secretary didn't have much on the ball.

"I could tell this made Bob feel especially uncomfortable, but what I liked about him was his willingness to come along just because he knew these events were important to me. Finally, we both decided they weren't worth the trouble. Long before we broke up, we'd stopped going out. To avoid making him feel uncomfortable, I'd spend most of my evenings at home with Bob."

It is important to keep in mind an important fact about romantic overachievement. Getting a date and having a relationship are different things. Both are difficult when approaching those who have a higher RMV; sustaining a relationship is more difficult. Individuals who attract and date those who appear to be above their RMV level are apt to have exceptional social skills. They are, for example, able to compensate for their lesser RMV attributes by having strong interpersonal strengths such as exceptional intelligence, charisma, sexual prowess, or humor. As a result they enjoy a good romantic ending, despite having been faced with low probability for success at the outset.

Just about everyone, however, considers himself or herself to be a romantic overachiever—though in reality most of us are not. Furthermore, many of those whom we believe to be overachieving romantically are not. They are most often merely compensating for their lesser RMV by contributing more to their romantic relationships than are their partners, in ways, or at times, that are unobservable to us. This might include consistently paying the car note of an extremely attractive girlfriend, or making child-support payments for that real hunk who always seems to be between jobs.

Are The RMV Of Men And Women Assessed Differently?

A black TV reporter I knew, who began as a "weather woman" at an independent station in the midwest, used to say she had two strikes against her in the competitive business of television news. First, she had difficulty because of her race, and second, she faced hurdles because of her gender. Women in television, according to her, were judged differently from men. "You see a man on the screen, past fifty and balding, and you hear women say he's a valuable catch because of the money he presumably makes," this woman lamented. "People see a woman past fifty on television and the only thing they judge her by are her looks. It's as if her looks are her only asset."

The only thing I can add to my friend's assessment is that what's true in the TV news business also applies to the black singles scene. Although black males and females by and large share the same RMV attributes, the order of the relative importance of these attributes tends to differ. For example, physical attractiveness continues to be the major attribute employed by most men in determining a woman's romantic desirability. In contrast, women give greater weight to a man's professional and economic status in determining his RMV. However, if black women continue to increase their professional clout, their financial portfolios may soon outweigh their looks in terms of romantic market importance. This is an increasing possibility as black men continue to lose economic ground, thereby making the earning potential of their partners of greater importance.

Should You Always Seek The Person With The Highest RMV?

Once again, despite the evidence from researchers that relationships go better when the partners are most evenly matched, there is always a tendency among people to seek the most that they can from the romantic marketplace. An alternative is to seek slightly less than your RMV suggests you might be able to command. This strategy may give you the advantage of having more comfort in your relationships because you do not have to overextend yourself, and should provide you with feelings of greater security.

This strategy of getting less of what would seem to be most desirable reminds me of how my dad always says he likes to buy his shoes. He, like most of us, doesn't want to appear to have big feet. He claims that he actually wears a size nine shoe, but that a size ten feels so good, he always buys a size eleven. I am not suggesting with this analogy that you get a partner who is unsuitable for you, or one you do not value—that is, one whose RMV is too different from your own. But I am suggesting that you try to find someone with whom you feel comfortable, and not necessarily the most sought-after individual in the marketplace, even if he or she is available. It may be most advantageous to resist the temptation to get the "most" in favor of finding what may be the "best": someone you feel is worthy of you, who is at the same time someone with whom you can feel relaxed. This less-aggressive romantic strategy sounds rather commonsensical. But it runs counter to the notion that we should always try to get the most we can, given what we've got. This idea goes down especially hard with people who are high achievers. They often have difficulty understanding that it may sometimes be beneficial to demand less than the maximum.

3 Identify Your Field of Eligibles

EVEN AFTER YOU'VE developed an accurate idea of your RMV, you may still be unsure of whom you should consider dating. You must decide who among those within your RMV range would be the best romantic partner for you. Choosing the right person is difficult because there are no "right" choices, only choices that seem right given what you want at the time. All choices have their pros and cons. One of the virtues of having dated a variety of people is that you have probably learned, rather painfully in some cases, what you *don't* want in a partner. However, this still leaves unanswered the question of what type of partner you *do* want. The problem may lie in your not having a sufficient grasp on what you *value*.

A good way to begin dealing with this problem is to step out of the romantic arena for a time and make a good, objective review of which personal qualities are most important to you in a partner. Some of these qualities are apt to be universally appealing, in that virtually everyone finds them desirable: honesty, warmth, sensitivity, kindness, genuineness. Others are less universal in their appeal but may well be important to you. Make as complete a list as possible, then judge how important each quality is to you using a scale running from desirable (but optional) to essential.

To get you started and to provide some ideas, review the hypothetical list below, but by no means limit your desires to the items present here. You must make your own list! No matter how brief or long, it will give you a more accurate picture of what you value and want in a partner.

It is important that my partner be:

Honest
Desirable   1 2 3 4 5 6 7 8 9 10   Essential

Ambitious
Desirable   1 2 3 4 5 6 7 8 9 10   Essential

Sensitive
Desirable   1 2 3 4 5 6 7 8 9 10   Essential

Highly sexual (likes frequent sex)
Desirable   1 2 3 4 5 6 7 8 9 10   Essential

Financially sensible (likes to save money)
Desirable   1 2 3 4 5 6 7 8 9 10   Essential

Religious
Desirable   1 2 3 4 5 6 7 8 9 10   Essential

Kind
Desirable   1 2 3 4 5 6 7 8 9 10   Essential

A Homebody
Desirable   1 2 3 4 5 6 7 8 9 10   Essential

A Sports fan
Desirable   1 2 3 4 5 6 7 8 9 10   Essential

Funny
Desirable   1 2 3 4 5 6 7 8 9 10   Essential

Family-minded (wants children)
Desirable   1 2 3 4 5 6 7 8 9 10   Essential

Civic-minded
Desirable   1 2 3 4 5 6 7 8 9 10   Essential

Good at communicating
Desirable   1 2 3 4 5 6 7 8 9 10   Essential

Sociable (likes to party and be with people)
Desirable   1 2 3 4 5 6 7 8 9 10   Essential

Athletic
Desirable   1 2 3 4 5 6 7 8 9 10   Essential

Once you have rated those qualities that you value in a partner, go back and rank-order them, with the highest-scoring quality first, the next-highest score second, and so forth. Carefully review your list. See what you most value in a partner by locating those qualities that make up the top half of your list. You would do best to focus your romantic attentions on potential partners who possess these qualities. It is with these people that you have the greatest probability of being most compatible. Obviously no one will possess all the qualities in the top half of your list, but it is not unrealistic that a partner should possess most of your most-valued attributes.

During one of my singles workshops, a number of men and women made comments about the many off-the-wall experiences they had incurred dating different types of people. None made this point as well as Stella, an aerobics instructor wearing an exercise outfit and a headband bearing a striking African motif. Stella walked in late, but she wasted no time in helping to set the tone of the workshop. Her comments revealed her tendency to cast such a broad romantic net that she ended up catching a number of unsuitable partners.

"I've dated all types of men," she said, then paused and turned to look at some of the other women in the audience, "including the type you're looking for. Everybody seems to want to date wealthy guys. Well, the ones I dated were always busy talking about making money, and they didn't mind spending it on me. Every time I got mad about something, they would buy me something, as if a gift would pacify me. I decided I didn't need a man who used money as a substitute for feelings."

Following these comments she got on the case of a particularly handsome man she had once dated, and although I wanted to go on with the workshop, nobody wanted to miss anything she had to say. Stella continued, "Some days, I'd do nothing but look at him," an edge of bitterness in her voice. "I mean he was just that good looking. I eventually realized that all he had to offer me were looks and conceit, because he hadn't taken the time to develop much of a personality or be interested in anything beyond himself. You know the saying that what you see is what you get? Well, if you fall for looks, that's about *all* you'll get."

She then made the roomful of men and women crack up with laughter when she got to her experience with dating younger men: "At first, I felt lucky because guys five to ten years younger than me found me attractive. I ain't no fool, now. I know a lot of them were just flirting. But there was this one guy named Tony who was real serious about taking care of business. And, honey, we had a ball. Especially in bed. It was important to him that I was satisfied. What he didn't know was that I couldn't help but be satisfied, because sex with him was absolutely out of this world. But I had to face up to the fact that Tony was like a lot of other young men. He was emotionally immature, unstable, and he thought being good in bed was all he needed to get through a relationship. I had to tell him that being well hung wasn't everything."

The audience was still howling when a man in his late fifties asked half in jest, "What about us older guys?" Stella didn't miss a beat: "Oh, I've dated plenty of your kind, too. For a hot minute, I thought I'd found the right balance between love, wisdom, and maturity in one older guy I was dating. But all that wasn't worth the trip he put me through. Why is it that you older guys talk to younger women like they're children? He tried to run my life! I found out the only thing he really knew how to run was his bath water. Plus, he was too sedentary for me. On Friday nights, after I close my exercise shop, I like to come home, unwind, and get ready to step out with my man around ten or eleven. By then, he was sound asleep."

Stella then shifted gears, turning her attention to men she derisively referred to as "inter-leck-shuls." "You wonder what happened to their brains," she went on. "I mean, they don't have the sense to know women don't want to spend every evening talking about world problems. I remember one guy in particular. A Morehouse professor. I met him at a Kappa dance. After we went out a few times, it occurred to me that he was good at analyzing life but didn't know a damned thing about living it."

Stella's dating experiences point out the potential ups and downs of making even the most basic decisions with respect to which attributes you most value in your romantic partners. Even when we think we know what we value, we are likely to experience some disappointment with our choice of partners. One possible remedy is to have a variety of partners who can complement our needs. Which is exactly what many dating singles do! The downside is that this shotgun strategy wears us down after a while, as it can be expensive, time consuming, and emotionally draining—and if we are sexually active, it can increase our probabilities of contracting sexually transmitted diseases.

However, knowing what you value should help you make better

romantic choices. It should also reduce the odds that you will continue to make the same mistakes in your choice of partners. In some respects the ideal romantic partner is like tomorrow: he or she always appears to be coming over the horizon but never arrives. But if you sort out your own values, you are more likely to get most of the things you want in a relationship. That's why it helps to determine your own values first. You're never happy for long when dating someone who doesn't suit your romantic preferences. Remember, your friends and family can advise you in clarifying your romantic values, but ultimately you must decide for yourself.

Should Black Women Alter Their Romantic Criteria?

Monica, a bright and energetic human resources manager at a local utility company, keeps fit by playing racquet ball at the gym where I work out. She gave me yet another excuse not to get on the stationary bike right away one evening when she asked if I might give her some advice. I had first met her at the gym months before, and it never occurred to me that she, a woman who seemed to have so much going for her in terms of looks and professional success, would encounter the problem she was facing in dating a man by the name of Ted. "It's a long story," she related. "My whole life centers around my work. I'm out of town at least two days a week at meetings that involve mostly white men. When I'm in conferences with them, I often wonder why there are so few black males holding professional jobs."

"So," I interrupted, "you're thinking about dating one of your white colleagues?"

"Well, not exactly. He's black. I met him not long ago when I stopped to pick up some fast food. He had on this white tennis outfit, and he gave me a look that made me feel a little insecure for a minute. Most men don't corner me that way. Anyway, while we were exchanging small talk, he sounded so intelligent and charming that I ended up giving him my number. My work number. I was a little disappointed when I found out he didn't exactly work downtown."

"In other words, he doesn't have a professional job," I said.

"But he's a real nice guy," she said defensively. "He's a welder. And I think I like him very much. After I learned what he did for a living, I was a little surprised that he wasn't exactly jumping with joy over the fact that he could possibly make it with a professional black woman like me. He called me at work a lot, but he sort of made it clear that he was in no hurry to ask me out. That hurt my ego a little, but I was pleased that he took an interest in me."

"So what's the problem?" I wanted to know.

"I don't mean to sound snobbish, but I just can't seem to decide whether I want to date a welder. He was bold enough to strike up a conversation and go for it, which is more than a lot of professional men have done. And he doesn't seem the least bit uncomfortable that I'm superior to him in terms of education and income. This town seems to have so few men at my level that I've been doing some serious thinking. I need to get out more, do something besides take business trips, exercise, go to church, and read. I'm thinking of dating Ted."

I knew she was hoping I'd say, "Go for it, Monica." But I couldn't give her a definitive response because I didn't know enough about the welder, or about Monica's private life, for that matter. But I did remind her that the question she raised—whether professional people should date only other professional people—is one that confronts many black singles. I pointed out that this issue is raised mostly in relation to professional black women. They are frequently urged to alter their standards for choosing romantic partners in order to enhance their chances of finding them. Given the low black male-female ratio, it is frequently suggested that black women should expand their definition of who is romantically acceptable. That is, they should break with the conventional criteria of male-female mate selection.

In the case of Monica and Ted, their differences in social, economic, and professional status have implications that put them at odds with prevailing cultural expectations. Those expectations hold that black men should focus their romantic pursuits on partners who are at or below their achieved level of social, economic, and professional status. As for black women, the cultural expectations are that they will seek romantic partners whose level of social, economic, and professional status is at their level or above. Hence, as men go farther up the social, economic, and professional pyramid, their field of romantic eligibles increases, while those for upwardly mobile women tend to decrease.

Monica's dilemma is one familiar to many professional women. Moreover, if the current educational imbalance for black males and females continues, Monica's experience will become even more commonplace. Although people tend to think of this issue as one that is problematic only for black women, the fact is that the educational and professional imbalance increasingly causes difficulties for both sexes. Black men too find themselves shying away from women they would actually like to date.

This imbalance between black men and women contributes to the popular point of view that black women should abandon the traditional criteria of mate selection. Many have suggested that black women should alter their romantic standards and consider men of lower educational and economic status. Black women are urged, not only for their own sake but for the sake of strengthening black families, to expect different things from their potential mates. For example, some advocate that these black women should evaluate romantic partners based on their ability to provide "genuine love" and caring for them and a family.

As you can see, people who hold this point of view place most of the onus on the romantic standards of black women. The assumption is that concessions by black women would help to reduce the matchmaking problems of black people. Such a strategy, while well-meaning, would not substantially reduce the problems experienced by black singles. For one thing, it would not have any effect on the shortage of black men. Instead, it would increase the likelihood of middle-class black women finding romantic partners while simultaneously decreasing the field of men available to working-class black women. In addition, urging women in Monica's position to change their romantic criteria also does not take into account the fact that black men have their own criteria; it is men, in most instances, who are the initiators of romantic activity. Note that it was Ted who first struck up a conversation with Monica and not the other way around. Thus, as Ted's behavior toward Monica shows, it's rather presumptuous to assume that working-class black men will rush to date women who have greater professional or economic status.

After all, the romantic market is very good for most employed black males, especially those who have mastered a trade and earn decent incomes, as was the case with Ted. There is an abundance of women who already fall within their criteria of "eligible." They may feel no great urgency to "date up." Instead they are probably inclined to ask themselves what they stand to gain by dating the better-educated and -salaried professional female. They may feel that although such women may have more resources, these women may not necessarily be willing to share those resources in a manner that would substantially affect them. This is not to mention the fact that some men may fear that they have something to lose in such relationships—power.

It is often said that some nonprofessional black men (and some professionals, too) feel threatened by professional women. "Threatened" may be the wrong term since it implies fear. It may be that they perceive romance with these better-educated, more financially secure women as potentially less advantageous to them, even if it may have the potential to be more financially rewarding. Those men who do enter into such relationships may believe that they are sacrificing power with no guarantee of greater personal satisfaction. Given their advantage in the romantic marketplace, some black men might well decide that the costs of pursuing professional women outweigh the benefits.

Is There A Solution?

There is no denying that some 30 percent of black families consist of females who earn more than their husbands. As I pointed out to Monica, the fact that there are so many black families in which the woman makes more money is a good sign that blacks only loosely adhere to mainstream society's traditional notion that the husband and father should be the chief breadwinner. The high percentage of black families in which this is not the case suggests that black singles can get along in situations where women have an equal or higher professional status than men.

For sure, the changing educational and professional levels of black men and women will affect their attitudes with respect to how they choose partners. Currently, however, there is a disparity between the realities of the situation and the attitudes prevalent among black people with respect to how couples match up. It is still considered acceptable for men to have partners who have less income and education than they, but this is also still considered less acceptable for women. While it is noble to suggest that black women break with tradition in selecting partners, doing so is still perceived by most of them as "settling."

There is a strong temptation to argue for abandoning what are thought to be "superficial" factors of mate selection, such as education and income. But unless you can reconcile the difference between what you have been told to expect in a person and what your actual romantic partner is actually like, you are likely to suffer unsatisfactory romantic experiences. For example, if you feel superior to your partner on the basis of having a higher RMV, then your attitude is likely to harm the relationship in the long run. That's why you and your partner must really believe in the correctness of your decision if you chose to abandon traditional beliefs about romance. If a relationship is to survive this break with social customs, a black couple must feel genuinely lucky to have each other.

The Dilemma: Security Vs. Excitement

We often hear our friends talk about how they are bored with their romantic partners, but then see them return to the romantic marketplace and find a partner just like their old one. Similarly, some people always complain that they keep dating "crazy" people, despite their stated desire for sane relationships. Both of these instances may reflect a value conflict.

Should you favor security over excitement or vice versa? The fact that one of these two qualities tends to be in short supply in any given individual means that you are likely to be forced to make a difficult choice. Everyone wants security, and to be able to count on their partners to behave in predictable ways. What we want is for them to be there when we need them. And yet, we still yearn for something extra. The researchers Hatfield and Walster, in their book *A New Look at Love*, suggest that "once we become really secure, we may stop focusing on what we have—security—and start longing for what we don't—excitement."

Our need for security is intuitively understandable; our need for excitement is less so. Most people, it seems, have an unexplainable desire to be exposed to new and novel stimulation, often in the form of unfamiliarity, uncertainty, and danger.

Thus in seeking romantic partners, you are frequently placing yourself in a dilemma—you want someone who can make you feel secure and still excite you. You want what you get from a carnival ride—excitement with little risk. The problem is that those behaviors that make us feel secure and those that excite us are inclined to be mutually exclusive.

People who excite us often offer little in the way of security. They tend to live on the edge of what is viewed to be safe. They are inclined to do and say things that, while exciting, might also make us feel a little nervous. And because we are less certain of their predictability, we may also be less certain of their long-term suitability for us. You are apt to find yourself in a classic situation, where the person who excites you most is the one you trust the least! If placed in an either/or situation, your need for security will probably win out over your desire for excitement.

Whichever side of the fence you come down on, you will probably continue to struggle with the liabilities of your romantic values. Since few partners, no matter how talented or versatile, will completely satisfy your need for both security and excitement, you probably should decide whether you will be more unhappy coping with repeated boredom or frequent nervousness. Whether you prefer excitement or security from a romantic partner will probably depend on your level of tolerance for which of these qualities you *don't* prefer. But it should eventually become clear to you that you are probably choosing partners who offer the personal quality you value most, even if your expressed desire is for the other. There appears to be no final solution to this dilemma, but it is beneficial for all of us to stay aware of our competing desires. This awareness keeps us in touch with the essential fact that the source of our dissatisfactions frequently resides within us, rather than within our romantic partners.

4 The Importance of Color and Beauty

O N THAT SATURDAY NIGHT in 1990 that Debbye Turner, Miss Missouri, strutted across the stage in Atlantic City at the Miss America pageant, many of my friends and I were glued to our television screens in St. Louis. Most of us doubted that she'd win in spite of her grace and beauty, but we took pride in seeing a "home-girl" dazzle the judges. I won't describe the pandemonium that erupted when Debbye garnered the crown. Nor will I dwell on the madness that occurred a year later when Debbye was succeeded by yet another brown-skinned woman.

It's an understatement to say that it's a remarkable feat for black women to win the Miss America pageant two years in a row. You don't have to know much about beauty pageants to realize that something had changed in the American psyche. Only a decade ago, the judges probably wouldn't have taken a second look at Debbye or her successor—not because they weren't beautiful, but because their skin was considered much too dark to represent this country's notions of beauty. That it took the Miss America pageant so long to recognize the beauty of dark-skinned black women says much about the role that color plays in American society.

Whites are not alone in having these feelings about skin color. Black people probably make finer distinctions regarding skin color among themselves than most other ethnic groups do. Spike Lee's movie *School Daze* calls attention to this fact. The movie is strikingly funny to most of us, though we might have felt uneasy with the color-confrontations between the light-skinned "wannabes" and dark-complexioned "jigaboos." There is much truth in Lee's observations. Some black sororities and fraternities have and still do engage in the very color snobbery depicted in the movie.

Needless to say, this type of discrimination borders on self-hatred, as a classic 1947 study by psychologist Kenneth Clark and his wife Mamie demonstrated. A significant number of black children at that time appeared to prefer white dolls to black ones, an indication of what most believe to be a lack of racial pride. That many black children feel comfortable embracing black dolls nowadays is testimony to their greater self-acceptance and self-esteem, thanks to the social revolutions of the 1960s and 1970s.

Nevertheless, skin color remains a major issue in the dating behavior of black singles. "The blacker the berry the sweeter the juice" and "Light, bright, and damn near white" are but two of a multitude of African-American expressions that call attention to our different feelings about skin color. Because of the considerable baggage that accompanies this issue, a few brief comments are necessary.

African-Americans' tendency to give preference to light skin is rooted in two historical factors. First, light skin more closely approximated the white standard of beauty, which, alas, many blacks adopted.

Second, light skin became associated with greater social status. This came about because many light-skinned black children were the offspring of former slave owners; because of this, they received better jobs, education, and life opportunities. Our society has thus historically treated light-skinned blacks more favorably, even those who weren't the offspring of former slave owners.

Although having light skin remains a romantic asset for some black females, this accident of birth also can be a liability. One of many black women who have had to come to terms with this fact is Clara, whose olive-colored complexion fits the description of what used to be called a "high yellow." In another time she might have been considered a perfect catch for most any up-and-coming, color-conscious black male, but that's not necessarily so in these times. A legal secretary who was born and reared in Lafayette, Louisiana, Clara became aware of the pitfalls of having a light complexion after completing her training at a business college in New Orleans and taking a job in a suburb of Indianapolis. Some whites in the town mistook her for one of their own, but blacks who frequented the places where she hung out in Indianapolis were under no such illusions about Clara's racial identity. They always knew she had plenty of soul, not least because of her tongue-in-cheek comments about pig feet being her favorite delicacy and from her soulful rhythm on the dance floor.

Clara never tried to hide her African-American roots. Her apartment was full of telling evidence, including a recent family reunion picture of herself surrounded by relatives of varying shades of black. Clara, moreover, had no trouble getting any brother she desired—except the one she wanted most. His name was Freeman, a dashing young committeeman with higher political ambitions. They got to know each other because, by chance, they took the same Friday evening flight to a Black Expo in Gary, Indiana one summer. They began dating, and most people (including Clara) assumed they would eventually get married.

Two Christmases ago, however, an influential community group persuaded Freeman to run for public office. He finally lined up enough political support to announce his candidacy. Soon afterward, he broke off his relationship with Clara, claiming that their relationship was taking up too much of his time. Though devastated, Clara accepted his decision.

Three days before the election—which Freeman won, by the way—Clara says she learned the truth: a campaign worker informed her that the romance had fallen victim to politics and racism. It turned out that some influential whites, whose support Freeman needed in the city-wide race, let it be known that they felt uneasy supporting a black candidate who appeared to be dating a white woman!

It's quite possible that Clara and Freeman might have broken off their relationship for any number of reasons at a later date. But her fair complexion didn't help matters during this crucial stage in Freeman's political career. For the first time in her life, Clara realized that having white features could be a curse in disguise.

Her experience is unique, but her problem is not uncommon. Many light-skinned women have similar horror stories about how their complexions have interfered with their pursuit of both life and romance. These women have had to come to terms with the fact that being "high yellow" ain't what it used to be for two primary reasons. The first is the influence of the black consciousness movement, which we alluded to earlier. This movement led blacks to take positive attitudes about Negroid features, such as darker skin color and coarser hair.

Second, skin color now plays a less central role in determining a woman's desirability as a romantic partner. Picking partners on the basis of how closely they approximate white standards of beauty in both color and physical features just ain't cool anymore. Openly exhibiting a color bias is no longer acceptable in most black social circles. While there is little doubt that color continues to exert an influence on the romantic choices of black singles, it now tends to be only sheepishly admitted to by most blacks.

These factors have placed light-skinned black women, like Clara, on the defensive. Some have tried to cope by dating very dark-skinned men. In doing so, they are either trying to establish a bond with all black people, or they're simply reacting to the problems they've encountered from having the sort of looks that are more identified with white culture than with their own. In essence, they may feel the need to affirm their blackness through their choice of partner.

Many women readers probably are saying, "But I've never given much consideration to the complexion of the men I've dated." That's true up to a point. Yet due to social conditioning, most black women and men—consciously or unconsciously—take skin color into account in their romantic relationships. Still, women who say they haven't aren't being entirely dishonest. What they mean is that skin color has been of lesser importance in assessing a man's RMV. They have placed higher value on a man's other romantic assets, such as his professional or social status. This reality is captured best by those who say that what black women want most "is a man with intelligence, a good education, and a solid bank account." This statement reinforces the point that a man's hue isn't his most important asset. That's not to say some black women don't exhibit signs of being "color struck," but this seems to be a less frequent occurrence than among black men.

How can we reduce the impact of skin color on our romantic relationships, and on our other human interactions as well? I put the question to Donna, a loquacious and intelligent sister whose smooth, chocolate-brown complexion resembles a Hershey bar. The owner of an arts and crafts shop on a busy street in Brooklyn, Donna told me that blacks are conditioned to believe the saying that blue-eyed blondes (or, in our case, fair-skinned, straight-haired "wannabes") always have the most fun.

"Blacks need to learn to turn off the TV," Donna said. "It's as simple as that. They need to get away from sources of entertainment that reinforce primarily white notions of beauty." She cited a number of alternatives—African-American and Third World newspapers, magazines, and art that aren't rooted in Eurocentric standards. In addition, she suggests that African-Americans take more interest in the theater, particularly plays and musicals told from black perspectives.

"That's the only way we're going to hold onto our self-esteem, or regain it if we've lost it. Some folks say they can't do without television and white newspapers. I don't quarrel with that. But what's wrong with supplementing that with material that gives us an appreciation of our culture and the variety of colors of the people in it?"

'Nuf said.

The Importance Of Beauty

This section isn't about the relationship between beauty and sex, but some brief comments about the two are worth noting in passing. There is little doubt that physical beauty is sexually arousing. Most men probably believe that more-attractive women have sex more frequently than other women. Even if they don't, it is not for the lack of men trying to encourage them to do so. It is perhaps of no surprise that more-attractive women are generally viewed to be more sexually stimulating than less-attractive women. However, it is noteworthy that some research has found that once women begin having sex with their partners, they are viewed as being more attractive by their partners than women of similar appearance who are not having sex with their partners. I do not want to suggest here that women should have sex more often (that's up to them), but rather I am pointing out how in this instance having sex with a partner seems to have a positive effect on our perceptions of them.

All of this indicates that we size up a prospective partner's physical attractiveness long before we do much else. Next to skin color, beauty is the quality we are most likely to notice as we consciously and unconsciously evaluate new prospective partners.

Whether our concept of beauty is based on Caucasian or Afrocentric standards, the fact is that it remains one of life's big inequities. Some people have it; some don't. Physical attractiveness, as I noted in Chapter One, acts as a major gatekeeper in that it significantly affects who we allow into our romantic lives. Our own perceived physical attractiveness may not determine where we end up in a romantic relationship, but it does appear to affect where and whether we get started.

In most situations, we size up people on the basis of skin color and beauty before we have the opportunity to learn much else about them, such as whether they are well meaning, have good interpersonal skills, or possess exceptional talents. Like it or not, if people are physically attractive, it significantly affects the initial impression they make. That's why some black singles who are physically appealing already have an advantage in the romantic marketplace.

Is Beauty Only Skin Deep?

It is often said that beauty is only skin deep, but it seems that most people perceive it as running clear to the bone. That's why handsome men and beautiful women tend to have more positive things thought about and attributed to them. For example, it appears that attractive people are more likely to be perceived as having better personalities, desirable spouses and sexual partners, greater material rewards, and more social and professional happiness. Not surprisingly, it also is assumed that attractive people are less likely to remain single, and will marry earlier than less-attractive ones. In short, they are the people that other people wish they looked like. When I made that point to Donna, the Brooklyn arts and crafts shop owner, she acted as if she'd suddenly gained profound insight into the psychology of African-American life.

"My god!" she exclaimed from behind the counter of her incense-fragrant shop. "No wonder there are so many beauty parlors and so much emphasis on style and fashions in this neighborhood." Indeed, the thriving beauty business would seem to suggest that people aren't taking any chances. They don't put much credence in the notion that "If you want to be happy for the rest of your life take an ugly one in your life."

Since most people, including blacks, are average looking, they have few illusions about marrying people whose looks are judged to be superior to their own—unless, of course, they have plenty of money or social status to enhance their RMV. The fact is that people in general tend to seek out partners who match their own level of attractiveness. Ever wondered why couples seem to look alike after they've remained married for fifty years? The consensus among researchers is that these partners actually looked alike from the start. That reinforces my point that people tend to be attracted to potential partners who are perceived to be fair exchanges on a number of scales—physical attractiveness being one of them.

Physically attractiveness is an asset, especially in the eyes of black men. It is not uncommon to hear them refer to a sister as a "fox" or describe her as being built like a "brick house." In contrast, women are more likely to emphasize the importance of their romantic partner's personality attributes, such as warmth, honesty, and intelligence. Although a man's physique is not unimportant to black women, it appears to be less of a preoccupation with them.

There are, of course, exceptions. It is sometimes said, for instance, that men aggressively pursue women for their physical attributes. Up to now, women have been aggressive in this respect only when they have possessed fame, fortune, and influence, and were seeking romantic partners to match their high-RMV status. My guess is that this will become more true of black women in general in the 1990s, because the social/economic roles of black men and women are becoming increasingly similar. I predict that black women will more aggressively seek out physically attractive men as a means of enhancing their statuses, just as most black men already do.

Male-female differences in the emphasis on beauty can be explained in a number of ways. First, the evidence suggests that men have a genetically derived preference for visual sensation, resulting in their having greater sensitivity to light and shape. In contrast, women are more advanced in the language-dominant areas of the brain.

Second, men are more inclined than women to use social relation-ships as a means to enhance their status, meaning a woman's level of attractiveness tends to be more important to men and their sense of self-worth. This partly explains why men like to be seen in the compa-ny of beauties comparable to Phylicia Rashad or Lena Horne. Fulfilling this desire seems to have a payoff beyond the personal gratification men gain by dating beautiful women. After all, men who are accompa-nied by attractive females are evaluated more favorably by other people than men who have unattractive partners.

Is There A Down Side To Being Beautiful?

As is often the case, too much of a good thing can cause problems. Beauty has its drawbacks. Although being physically attractive is gener-ally a romantic advantage, it doesn't follow that being *exceptionally* attractive leads to even greater romantic advantages.

Exceptionally attractive people are sometimes intimidating to oth-ers. As a result they may actually be approached less often than people who are not as attractive. It seems that many people, out of fear of rejection, are sometimes reluctant to approach those who are consid-ered exceptionally attractive. While most of us would like to date peo-ple as attractive as Whitney Houston or Mario Van Peebles, we are inclined to view them as being so attractive as to be out of our league. In our efforts to protect ourselves from the trauma of rejection, we may not ask them to dance or to join us for drinks after work. In fact, we may even attempt to make a preemptive strike; that is, we may reject exceptionally attractive people before they have the opportunity to reject us. For example, we may go so far as to avoid getting into situa-tions with them where they might even think that we are going to approach them romantically. This sometimes leaves the exceptionally attractive people out in the cold.

Take the case of Angela. A former student at the university where I teach, Angela has muffin-brown skin, long brown hair, bright eyes—and a million dollar smile. You would think that with physical attri-butes like these, all would go well for Angela romantically. Not so! She states that she hardly has any female friends and that when she goes out to discos, she often is not approached by anyone. She reasons that prospective dates probably avoid her because she doesn't look like the average black person. She frequently finds herself in a bind for companionship as other women often don't want to accompany her to social outings—for fear, it seems, that she will be too powerful a romantic competitor. By the same token, if she goes out with her best male friend, Andre, other guys don't approach her because they assume that she already is involved with someone. Angela describes the situation as a frustrating one. This situation doesn't affect most "beautiful people," but many of them have experienced something like it at some point in their lives.

In some cases, very attractive people fail to develop the social skills and patience necessary to sustain romantic relationships. Because they often have an array of romantic options, they may be inclined to give up quickly and move on to another partner when a relationship turns stormy. A history of such behavior may result in their never learning the interpersonal skills necessary to sustain long-term romance. It is also sometimes the case that very attractive individuals fail to develop socially (and perhaps even emotionally) because so little has been asked of them, other than just to be beautiful. Subsequently, they may fail to develop more as people, which sometimes results in their coming off as shallow in relationships.

Another downside to being exceptionally beautiful is that it automatically creates resentments. Even before exceptionally attractive men and women are properly introduced to a group of new people, they may have already made enemies. I refer to this as the "I hate you already" phenomenon—they are often evaluated negatively by people they have never even met. It seems that these negative evaluations may be most severe among women. Furthermore, the negative attributions made to them are apt to vary with the attractiveness of the evaluator. Attractive women, when evaluated by less attractive women, are more likely to be perceived as being vain, likely to engage in extramarital affairs (to which there is some statistical truth), and more "bourgeois" as compared to unattractive women. While many may assume that such behavior occurs just between women, don't kid yourself; it occurs among men as well.

Perhaps the major implication for both men and women who are frequent victims of the "I hate you already" phenomenon is that they are likely to be invited to fewer social functions. Their exceptional level of attractiveness, in this instance, limits their social exposure and hence their opportunities to meet romantic partners. Being exceptionally attractive, then, is a mixed blessing. It can be a powerful asset, a magnet for luring and retaining romantic partners. It can also be a disadvantage, especially when jealousy comes into play.

Although most of us are just average looking, our looks need not be a barrier to success in the romantic marketplace, as we're more likely to date people whose attributes are similar to our own. This means that trying to remake yourself into a beauty queen or king isn't the best strategy for enhancing your romantic life. You are better off focusing less on attaining what you perceive as ideal beauty—changing your eye color by wearing contact lenses, for example—and more on improving your natural attributes.

The key isn't to expend energy trying to embellish yourself in unrealistic ways, but to change things over which you have immediate control. Doing so will make you a more pleasant and healthy human being, not only in your eyes but in the eyes of that someone whom you view as a potential romantic partner.

5   The Right Place

A S A KID I was never very good at basketball. I was neither tall enough nor quick enough to make the starting team. But one thing I did learn was that the best jumper didn't always get the rebound. Rather, the ball frequently fell into the hands of the players who knew best how to position themselves under the rim. The same kind of strategy comes in handy when looking for romantic partners. Learning to position yourself advantageously is one of the best skills you can acquire. One of the better examples of this strategy is employed by men at most nightspots. Have you ever noticed how men frequently gather near the women's restroom? Well, they do. And they do so because they are aware that a some point in the evening every woman in the club will make at least one trip past them on her way to freshen up. These men who wait in "ambush" by the restroom are strategically placing themselves in the way of romantic opportunities.

There are basically two schools of thought on finding romance. One contends that romance will come to you whether you look for it or not. The other holds that you must go out and find it. Although there is some validity to both strategies, it's probably evident that I lean toward taking a more active stand. While I do believe it's possible to try too hard—namely by saying and doing things that offend or scare off prospective partners—I also believe that the act of looking for romance increases the probability of finding it. In fact, when I ask singles who appear to be successful in finding romance to tell me their secret, most respond the way Mario did. Mario is a tall, dark-skinned, average-looking, thirty-five-year-old insurance salesman, who always has a story to tell and a smile to lay on you.

Mario has many physical attributes that make him naturally attractive to women—among them, a presence that reminds me somewhat of Wesley Snipes. On the basis of our basketball analogy, however, he (like me) might be regarded as being unlikely to make the starting team. Yet, he seems to have more success dating than men who appear to have higher RMVs than he does. Quite frankly, many men are better looking and have more going for them professionally than Mario. He says that the reason he is so successful is because he consistently makes the active effort to make romance happen. Mario is proof that people who seem to have plenty of dates are typically no different than those who don't, except for one fact: those who date frequently are simply more persistent and deliberate in their romantic game plan.

You must work at positioning yourself better in the romantic marketplace. This requires that you first locate your field of romantic eligibles (see Chapter Three). Black magazines and periodicals often list the cities that are thought to be best for meeting black singles. Typically, the list includes only the biggest cities, such as Los Angeles, Chicago, Detroit, New York, Philadelphia, Atlanta, and Washington D.C. Although most lists of where to find black singles usually include few cities besides Atlanta in the southern states, the geographical distribution of black people is now about equally divided between the North and the South. Hence, any number of southern cities provide a good place to meet eligible black singles. Charleston, Nashville, and, of course, New Orleans are all progressive cities with sizable black populations that offer plenty of romantic prospects. By the same token, you are probably wise to avoid moving to places like Wyoming or North Dakota (no matter how good the job offer!) if you hope to find a black romantic partner, as places such as these are apt to have very few.

For sure, some cities offer greater opportunities for meeting certain types of people than others. For example, Washington D.C. offers perhaps your best opportunity to meet an attorney. However, other cities may offer greater prospects for you to meet a more diverse group of potential partners. Atlanta, for example, has a large, well-established, and diverse black population. It is also important to remember that people in different parts of the country may have different values. For example, an *Ebony* magazine article once asked whether southern men made better husbands. While the answer to this question is that it depends upon a number of factors, the article did suggest that if you prefer a more traditional male with respect to gender roles, then the South is perhaps the best place to find that sort of man. The point is that whenever looking at the merits of a particular city, you should consider factors other than the raw numbers of black males or females who live there. Look also at the cultural and social factors that will help you determine whether a certain city might have many of the types of partners you are seeking.

Is Bigger Better?

I want to offer a word of advice on the "numbers" of black men and women in any given city. The numbers are just that—numbers. Although they give some indication of your probability of meeting black men and women in a given city, they do not automatically seal your romantic fate. After all, romantic singles beat the romantic odds every day. Take the case of Nancy, a native Atlantan in her early forties. An accountant, Nancy had a job offer from an aircraft parts manufacturer. The position required her to relocate to St. Louis. Her friends told her to refuse to relocate despite the fact that the offer amounted to a substantial advancement in her career. She took the job and still remembers her friends saying, "Honey, you'll never find a man if you leave Atlanta." Much to their surprise, less than a year after moving to St. Louis, Nancy found and married a guy who also worked for the aircraft company. It seems that he had been in St. Louis for five years and hadn't dated anyone seriously until he met Nancy. The chances of these two black people meeting in a company that was overwhelmingly white was, to use Nancy's expression, "a miracle." But it happened, and it happens all the time.

It's true that where there are more people, there are more prospective partners. Yet, the larger the city, the more likely we are to find singles advertising in the local newspapers for partners. It is possible that people in smaller towns would like to advertise too, but choose not to out of fear that they might be labeled freaks and weirdos by their small-town (and perhaps small-minded) neighbors and friends.

But whatever the case, it is clear that just being in a bigger city is not in itself the answer to finding romance. In fact, large cities can be tougher places to get to know people; I'm sure that comes as no surprise to those who live in very large cities, such as New York or L.A. For black singles, the transition from stranger to friend in large cities is likely to be difficult for three reasons: people are busier and have less time and energy to develop friendships; they are fearful of crime and, hence, more apprehensive about meeting strangers; and, since getting around in a big city can be so complicated, it is often too difficult to reach the places where they can find those with whom they would like to have more social contact. However, black singles who do live in large cities are at least likely to enjoy more superficial contact with a wider variety of potential romantic partners—which tends to keep hope alive.

There are pros and cons, then, to moving to a big city. On the one hand, the sheer numbers of potential dates and mates is definitely an advantage. On the other hand, smaller towns may offer a greater probability of meeting those prospects who are available. Unfortunately, there is no clear-cut answer to this dilemma. If you are trying to decide if you should move from a small city to a larger one, you should also take into consideration how good you think you are at making new friends. If you tend to be outgoing and engaging, the disadvantages may be minimized. If you are not good at breaking into new social settings, then a small or medium-sized city may be your best choice. Needless to say, having family and friends in a city is an invaluable resource. This factor, too, should be weighed heavily in your decisions.

For better or worse, most of us do not have the option to move to another city anyway. Because we are faced with other priorities, most notably the need to earn a living, moving is most likely to occur only if we are transferred or are offered employment at another location. However, even if the number of eligibles in your city doesn't look good, all is not lost. It is not necessary to find a whole city teeming with potential partners. Remember, all you need to do is find just one—the right one!

Where Do We Meet People?

Your aim is to place yourself in the way of romance, and that can mean just about everywhere you go. Often people meet romantic partners at places that seemingly have nothing to do with romance. Aside from making new acquaintances at the traditional singles places—night clubs, parties, weddings (ideally not your own)—people can also meet prospective partners while carrying out everyday activities.

It is a well-known fact that grocery stores have become, in some instances, real "meat markets," as people now hope to make friends while shopping. Shopping provides an excellent opportunity to meet new people. It offers the chance for a number of brief encounters in which people can make repeated visual or verbal contact without making any commitments. Romantic hopefuls can ask each other for assistance in a way that leads to further communication. Moreover, because shopping is likely to be repeated in the same stores, there exists the possibility for future meetings. Somehow, a second meeting or sighting always seems to make communication between strangers easier.

For women, a casual stroll through the men's department in a clothing store might turn up prospects; men, meanwhile, might stroll through the women's department in their search. A simple question, whether honest or contrived—"Pardon me, but do you think that this size would fit my brother/sister?"—might be enough to spark a conversation. Moreover, don't overlook salespeople. Many of them are single and take sales jobs not only as a source of income, but also because it gives them a chance to get out and meet new people.

Shopping is but one of many regular activities that afford you the opportunity to meet potential partners. Many black men and women who are single belong to religious, social, and community organizations where they might possibly find romance. If you have children, attend your local PTA meetings, and find out if your community has such groups as Parents Without Partners, whose meetings you might want to attend. Groups such as the Big Brothers and Big Sisters, community theaters, the Urban League, the NAACP, and black professional groups are all excellent places to seek romance while at the same time doing a little good for your neighbors. For sure, you won't be the first person to find romance while helping others. The good thing about meeting a partner through your mutual participation in an organization or civic cause is that you'll know that you already share some things in common.

Of course, each town has its own special groups and activities. A good place to find out where things are happening is your community's black newspapers and entertainment guides. If there isn't a local black publication where you live, try contacting black civic groups or religious leaders. They are generally good sources of information. Finally, you might find yourself a popular barber shop or beauty salon. The owners and regular customers are almost always in-the-know as to what's happening in the black community.

Whatever you do, don't overlook the obvious. You may find that in many instances, all you have to do is notice those who already have noticed you! I mentioned in Chapter One that Cupid is best suited for short flights, and that you are most likely to date those who live, work, or play close by. Keep in mind that most of the *opportunities* you have to establish romantic relationships occur in situations that have little or nothing to do with your explicit attempts to find partners. It is because of this that many people attest to finding romance when and where they least expected it. Your most mundane activities, such as visiting a sick friend in the hospital or picking up dry cleaning, are potential opportunities to make romantic acquaintances. By recognizing this fact, you will become more conscious of the opportunities these basic day-to-day activities afford, and you will simultaneously enhance your prospects of making social contacts with people who otherwise would remain strangers. So don't limit your efforts to Friday and Saturday nights.

"Haven't I Seen You Some Place Before?"

This overused method of self-introduction has a good track record. Whether the question is legitimate or merely a ploy, the frequent favorable responses to it attests to the importance of what psychologists refer to as "mere exposure." We are inclined to be attracted to people we've had prior exposure to. It is commonly said that familiarity breeds contempt. But the fact is that we are more apt to like people (or things) who are familiar to us. There is something about people we have seen before, even if only briefly, that sets them apart from those we have not. Even a very brief visual contact reduces our sense that someone is a stranger—when, for all practical purposes, he or she is. So, not only is it a good idea to be seen by those you want to like you; it is even better for them to see you repeatedly.

If possible you should try to get yourself introduced. This may require that you introduce yourself, or have someone else introduce you. While you must not become offensive in your efforts to be seen by someone, having pleasant repeated contacts with him or her is likely to work in your favor.

My Place, Your Place, Or An Exciting Place

Once a new acquaintance agrees to a date with you, you are confronted with the question of where to go. The setting of your initial romantic encounter is particularly important because it is part of your first impression. Like other aspects of your first impression, what you do on a first date is likely to have considerable impact on whatever future dates take place—if they take place. For sure, you want to go some place that will promote your romantic intentions. Most of us are inclined to take our dates to our favorite places, but these places may have little power to promote romance if they fail to interest or excite our dates. Finding a mutually enjoyable place and activity for you and your partner has a good chance of fostering romance, since you are most likely to establish lasting friendships with partners whose interests and tastes are similar to your own. In fact, the desire to partake in similar pastimes is believed to be a good predictor of the success of the relationship. It seems that those who play together are more apt to stay together.

Clearly some places and activities have a greater probability of promoting romance than others. A company picnic, for instance, is likely to be a poor choice for a first date. Such an activity might interfere with you and your date having sufficient privacy to get to know each other. Yet, selecting a place that is too intimate also can be a mistake. For example, a candlelit dinner may be too much too soon. In addition to costing a bundle, this type of date can be a flop. Keep in mind that, on a first date, your partner is likely to experience what's known as "approach-avoidance." In such cases, he or she may have a strong desire to approach you, while feeling at the same time an equally strong impulse to retain some physical and emotional distance. While very romantic, a candlelit dinner may also turn out to be too intimate and a little too intense for the first date. Placing a new date in a situation where he or she is required to interact with you too intimately too soon may serve to activate your date's approach-avoidance reaction.

Hence, try to find initial dating activities that require low levels of intimate interaction. Providing this delicate balance is what makes going to the movies so popular. The movie theater setting is almost a form of what child psychologists call "parallel play." In other words, you and your new date are able to do something together, but at the same time do it rather independently of the other. Going to the movies affords the opportunity for close proximity and some brief expressions of feelings, such as anger, fear, or laughter.

Finally, despite the fact that we often think of romantic places as being dimly lit and serene, research evidence suggests that a more exciting, stimulating place also may enhance our romantic (and even sexual) attraction to others. Because our bodies often have difficulty identifying the exact source of the sensations we experience, they frequently rely on the context or environment for clues. In other words, we may turn to our immediate surroundings to help us explain what we are feeling at a particular moment. Indeed, there is some evidence suggesting that a man meeting a woman under stimulating circumstances is more likely to perceive her as being romantically desirable than if he meets her in more mundane circumstances. It seems that the stimulation generated from an exciting situation is associated with the person who shares the situation with you. So you may want to explore first dates that involve some sort of exciting, emotionally arousing activity. Attending a lively social, political, or sporting event, or engaging in a dynamic leisure activity such as horseback riding, may not only result in the two of you having a good time, but also may lead your date to conclude that you are an exciting and attractive romantic partner.

In my view, it may be unwise to resort automatically to quiet walks and calm conversations on first dates. While these activities may contribute to your being perceived as kind, sensitive, and a great source of comfort, these activities may not stir up a great deal of passion and excitement. They might even contribute to you being perceived as more of a "buddy" than a romantic partner. And as some of you already know, there are few things more frustrating than becoming somebody's buddy, when what you really want is romance. You are likely to lose nothing by being perceived as an exciting, sexually attractive person. So, attempt to heat up your dating endeavors with activities that will pump up and excite your potential partners.

6 The Right Time

TIMING IS TO FINDING ROMANTIC RELATIONSHIPS what location is to buying real estate—everything! Meeting partners and establishing relationships are often as much a function of timing as anything else. We have all met individuals interested in dating us when we were involved in other relationships or with other issues, such as jobs or personal crises. Similarly, most of us have wanted to establish a romantic relationship with a person who turned out to be dating someone else. If and when that person became available, we too were dating someone else.

Actually, you can never have any significant control over the romantic timing of others. However, having an awareness of where you are with respect to your own romantic timing should assist you in your romantic selections. The real question is: Where are you in your desire for a dating relationship? Knowing where you are with respect to your own romantic timetable and having an understanding of your romantic possibilities will reduce your frustrating search for the right person. Also, by having greater insight into how timing affects romance, you will understand better your romantic past, and be more in control of your romantic future.

Timing and Partners

With respect to timing, your relationships are most likely to fall into one of four categories: right partner/wrong time; wrong partner/right time; wrong partner/wrong time; and right partner/right time. Let's review these four romantic possibilities.

Right Partner/Wrong Time

Many of us have met people we felt would have made good romantic partners, but at a time when we were unable to accommodate them. In this respect, some of the romantic partners with whom we would most like to have a serious relationship have already come and gone from our lives. We probably remember them as being the best candidates we have ever met. These are the people about whom we say, "If only I could meet him (her) today." Unfortunately, we met them when our own situations or circumstances were not conducive to establishing a relationship—at least, not with them. Maybe we were already attached. Or perhaps we were either too young (if not immature), in the military, away at college, or engaged in some other endeavor that was not conducive to establishing a romance. Kenny, a friend of mine who looks a lot like the boxer Thomas Hearns, told me the following story:

One winter afternoon in December, as he was on his way to Kansas City to visit his fiancee, his connecting flight out of St. Louis was delayed because of a fierce snowstorm. In the airport crowd of weary-looking air travelers, he couldn't help but notice an attractive African-American woman leaving a ticket counter and heading for a terminal chair to wait out the long layover. Sitting down beside her, Kenny struck up a conversation and found her to be pleasant and as open to conversation as he. Her name was Marilyn; she was unattached, he learned, and was headed for Florida to spend Christmas with her parents. As they talked, Kenny said he sensed a mutual attraction. The thing that stood in the way was the fact that he was engaged, and very much in love with his fiancee.

"Visibility at the airport was so poor that flights couldn't land or leave until the next day," Kenny recalled. "But somehow I didn't feel the least bit inconvenienced over being stranded. Luckily, Marilyn and I were put up over night in the same hotel and got to spend even more time together. Man, the place was just perfect for romance. It had a nightclub and a piano bar, and this brother who sang love ballads I hadn't heard in years. He really made us forget about the layover and the dreary weather. We each went back to our separate rooms after midnight, and she flew on to Florida the next morning. I loved my wife when she was my fiancee and I still love her today. But on my flight to Kansas City the next morning, I kept wondering why I was destined to meet such a fine woman just when I was about to marry somebody else."

Wrong Partner/Right Time

Kenny, of course, could have been in a worse situation, one in which he had met the wrong person at the right time. That is, he might have been ready for romance with a person who was not ready for him! This type of situation is apt to be hazardous to your romantic happiness. The wrong partner/right time situation causes the most pain, because you are inclined to try harder and have greater romantic expectations. My friend Marty once told me that when people decide the time is right for a serious romantic relationship, they tend to become "unwise romantic consumers"; because they feel the time is right to settle down into an in-depth dating relationship (if not marriage), they become less critical in their evaluations of potential partners. They are likely to begin thinking less about the qualities that their romantic partners actually possess, and more about what they want to have happen at this point in their lives. Many people decide that the time is right to settle down when they reach some milestone or plateau in life, such as achieving a long-sought professional goal. Others experience a nagging feeling that they are getting old, and should thus think more long-term about life and relationships.

For example, turning thirty was a traumatic event for Melba, a very outgoing, attractive social worker who was making great strides in her career. But her professional success seemed to pale next to the fact that she didn't have a serious romantic relationship. She wanted very much to get married and raise a family. Her main prospect was David, a high school band director. With good-natured humor, their friends would tease the couple about tying the knot; but David always politely but firmly shrugged off such comments with an air that he was in no rush to settle down. David eventually confided in Melba that the real stumbling block was his professional goal. He wanted to work full-time on a doctorate in music. He told her the graduate fellowship he had been assured of getting would barely support one person. Melba volunteered to supplement her income by working part-time as a counselor. It took another year for her to convince David that marriage wouldn't interfere with his academic plans, and the two were finally wed. The couple even had two children before David eventually completed his doctoral dissertation. They are now both successful. David recently was promoted to director of music for his entire school district. Melba's case is one where patience paid off.

Unlike Melba, some singles decide that the time is right for a steady partner following a series of short-term romantic relationships. They may simply decide that they've had enough brief romantic encounters and would like to establish a more meaningful relationship. Once they make that decision, they tend to work harder on their next romantic opportunity. Herein lies danger. We may decide (consciously or unconsciously) to fall in love with the next prospective partner we meet, irrespective of how unsuitable this person might be. Making such a decision is likely to result in unpleasant consequences.

Take Lisa's case. After graduating from Memphis State, she became a real estate salesperson and earned a comfortable living. When time permitted, she hung out with her friends, all of whom—save Harold— eventually got married. Lisa never had found Harold attractive, spoke in negative terms about him to her girlfriends, and kept her distance whenever he sought to begin a romantic relationship with her. She eventually moved to New York, where she lived for five years, and used to hang out in an uptown nightspot called Sweet Water's after work. She began to spend even more time there after her steady walked out, leaving her feeling she'd lost her only chance in the world to find a suitable romantic partner. However, one Friday afternoon, to Lisa's surprise, Harold walked into Sweet Water's. A journalist, he was in town for a convention. Lisa probably surprised him because she walked up and gave him a big hug as soon as he stepped in the door, presumably making him feel as though he was the most important person in the world. The truth was, Lisa was glad to see someone from "down home," as she put it.

They later corresponded, and Lisa eventually decided to move back to Memphis. Friends of her told me they were all blown away upon hearing she was dating Harold, a man she hadn't given five minutes of her time in the good old days. She'd obviously picked him out of desperation, they reasoned. When Lisa and Harold were seen together at social events in Memphis, her friends swore the relationship wouldn't last. Though events may prove them wrong, Lisa's sudden attraction to Harold may eventually wear thin.

Unfortunately, Lisa's situation of the wrong partner/right time scenario is common. And since we are likely to invest heavily in these relationships because of our desire to make them last, they are often easier gotten into than out of. Thus, when you feel the time is right, be especially cautious in your selection of a romantic partner.

Wrong Partner/Wrong Time

Relationships involving the wrong partner at the wrong time probably characterize the bulk of your romantic involvements. Most of us have found ourselves dating someone whom we realized wasn't *the* man or woman for us, even though he or she appealed to us. In addition, we may have felt that even if he or she *were* Mr. or Ms. Right, it wouldn't matter since we ourselves were not yet ready for a serious romance. Wrong partner/wrong time relationships are often brief because the parties perceive themselves as being able to offer too little to sustain a long-term relationship. On the other hand, if you meet the wrong partner at the wrong time, things could work out very nicely for a while. It helps if you are also not quite the person this prospective partner is looking for either. Of course, the two of you must at least like each other enough to enjoy one another's company, but you both also realize this relationship "ain't the one," since neither of you is looking for a serious relationship.

I know a couple, Brenda and Alfred, whose circumstances fitted the wrong partner/wrong time scenario. He worked in the credit department of an auto manufacturer and she was employed by a housing authority. I laughed a lot as I listened to Brenda explain how they met and then sustained their improbable relationship. Brenda said she came across his name while half-reading a singles column in a weekly newspaper. The ad, Brenda recalled, said: "BM [black male], average looking, enjoys outdoor activities, gourmet cooking, bicycling, and jazz." Brenda said that she was about to stop reading because "I assumed this would be another case of a brother looking for one of them AWBs—average white broads." But not Alfred, she said. He was seeking a "SBF [single black female] who desired occasional company." Her expectations weren't high. But just for the fun of it, she said she answered the ad and convinced some girlfriends to join her during the happy hour where she was to meet Alfred for the first time. He told her he'd be wearing a camel-colored blazer, but she misled him about what she'd be wearing just in case she chickened out. During the happy hour, she and her girlfriends decided that the broad-shouldered guy sitting at the bar in the camel-colored jacket was more handsome than his four-line advertisement made him out to be. Brenda said she summoned the courage to introduce herself to him, and he came over to their table and bought drinks for everybody.

"At least I knew he wasn't stingy," Brenda joked. Initially, both Alfred and Brenda decided they were not a good match. It seems that they had some rather important value differences about major issues such as religion, money, and politics. In particular, Alfred wanted to raise his children Muslim with the possibility of joining the Nation of Islam. Brenda, although quite religious, was from a long line of Baptist families and had no desire to convert to Islam. However, they continued to have plenty of fun together, cooking exotic dishes, bicycling in the spring, attending football games in the fall and social events throughout the year. Since they were unattached and weren't quite ready to commit themselves to finding new relationships, they realized that their temporary arrangements were perfect, allowing each to have a pleasant partner for social and other types of functions.

This couple's experiences show that, contrary to our preconceptions, wrong partner/wrong time relationships can be less painful than we might imagine. Most importantly, our desires and expectations for these relationships are lower, and thus we are less likely to be disappointed or frustrated if things don't work out. Brenda's relationship with Alfred was emotionally rewarding in that it offered both of them time to relax and chill out (we all know that serious relationships always require a great deal of work).

We might view such relationships as "coasters." In other words, we can ride along without too much pressure on the pedal rather than always being consumed in the heat of a romantic relationship. Furthermore, wrong partner/wrong time relationships can be fun if we accept them for what they are. The problem often is that most of us are inclined to try to date whomever we believe is the "right" person, even in periods when it's the wrong time for us. We do this as a sort of insurance, just in case we change our minds and find ourselves feeling it's the right time after all. However, given that so much of our romantic lives is spent in wrong partner/wrong time situations, it would probably be beneficial to learn to enjoy these situations and appreciate them for what they have to offer, if the person is not *too* wrong.

The experience of Brenda and Alfred indicates that the wrong partner/wrong time situation doesn't have to be unpleasant. In these relationships you may find it easier to get along with your partner because you are expecting, if not demanding, less. Recognizing this situation for what it is may provide you with a sort of time-out from your normal struggles to make your romantic life perfect.

Right Partner/Right Time

This is the situation most of you are looking for. Here it all comes together. Anyone who has dated has fantasized about finding the special person just when the time seems right. Doing so is no easy feat. It may have as much to do with your luck as with your astuteness as a romantic consumer. For sure, you have more influence on creating the right time than on conjuring up the right person. Yet, as we have seen in the lives of many of our friends and relatives, the two—the right partner and right time—do, quite frequently, arrive together.

7 Getting Off To a Good Start

THE BEGINNING OF ANY ROMANCE is particularly important because it offers us hope—hope that, at last, we have met the one. It is not just the novelty of a new relationship that excites most people, but rather the possibility that their new date might just be their future mate. Good romantic relationships, statistically speaking, are likely to have gotten off to good beginnings. Your first few encounters with a new dating partner are likely to be critical in determining the relationship's course.

The first impression others make on us strongly affects our desire to see them again. Similarly, the first impression we make on others influences their willingness to see us again. It is because good beginnings so often beget good endings that we are amazed when our friends and relatives tell us stories about how they and their partners didn't like each other when they first met, and how they later went on to establish a great romance. We've all heard stories that begin with something like, "I couldn't stand George when I first met him, because he thought he was so cute," or "Our first date was so terrible that I swore I'd never go out with her again." Anecdotes such as these make fascinating dinner conversation because of their uniqueness.

Don't expect cases like these to occur very often, though, because they don't! In fact, if someone makes a poor impression on us during our first date, we are unlikely to date that person again, unless circumstances somehow encourage or promote another date. Moreover, even if we have a chance to interact with that person later, we are likely to experience difficulty altering that initial impression. A first impression is difficult to change and is likely to be long lasting. Think of the people of whom you had bad first impressions, and how often it seems that you have retained that negative feeling about them even years later. All this suggests you should remember that, as the saying goes, "You don't get a second chance to make that first impression."

In addition, we are inclined to ignore evidence that is contrary to our initial appraisal of a person. If after a first date your prospective partner judges you to be a good person, you have increased significantly the probability of that person wanting to date you again. What you say, how you look, and what you do in your initial meeting with others has considerable impact. Try to remember that your first date is probably your most important one. Thus, if you are a charming, intelligent, well-groomed, caring, and witty person, be sure to express all of those qualities on a first date.

Even though the importance of "dressing well" as a factor in the dating process can be overemphasized, looking your best is important. Also, though there are potentially negative implications involved in the giving of extravagant gifts, flowers or some other token gift on the first date may help substantiate the fact that you are the good person that you really are. James, the former director of the African and Afro-American Studies department at the university where I teach, once told me that the woman who is now his wife brought a pie to his house on one of their first dates. He told me that he thinks he has loved her ever since.

Saying positive things is also likely to result in your being perceived as a more positive person. Never use "lines." Don't say things that aren't true—your compliments should always be sincere. This is actually very easy to do. Simply note those things that you find attractive about your date. Everyone has positive and unique attributes, such as their posture, hands, mustache, eyes, feet, smile, or teeth. Remember too that compliments addressing qualities over which a person has control—such as what they say, think, or do—have greater impact than compliments on factors over which the person may not have control, such as their level of physical attractiveness. Attempt to make your compliments as specific as possible; generic (one size fits all) compliments are less appreciated. For example, telling your dates that they are beautiful or handsome is apt to be less appreciated than telling them that you like what they have to say, or their ideas, or the choice of colors in their homes, or the way they carry themselves.

Even if you feel the urge, do not over-compliment your partners upon first meeting them. Excessive compliments have a tendency to lose their impact and sound phony. If you pay your partners what they perceive to be excessive compliments, they may soon come to believe that you are not very discriminating in your judgments, and that you probably say the same sorts of things to every potential partner you meet.

First Conversations
(To Be Or Not To Be Superficial)

Initiating and sustaining initial conversations with new people can be difficult. Yet your first conversation with a potential romantic partner is crucial. Just how crucial is made clear in the case of Tom, an aircraft assembly line worker, who told me of being turned off by Abby, a woman who initially seemed like a good catch because of Tom's attraction to what he called her "Third World" look. Her skin, he said, was smooth as fine leather and her brown eyes seemed to communicate with him even as she bit into a sandwich, as she ate lunch at a table ahead of him at a fast-food restaurant. He was taken by her especially long cornrows, girdled by a piece of cloth bearing an African print.

"But there was one thing that turned me off," Tom remembered with an air of disappointment. "I talked my way over to her table, and it didn't take me long to realize that Abby wasn't a woman I wanted to get to know well. She began telling me intimate things about herself that I didn't care to know right away. She was unattached, and she mentioned very casually all the bad things her former boyfriend had done to her and all the humiliating things she'd tolerated from him. She even told me she'd had an abortion for him. I might have warmed up to her if she'd waited a little longer to talk about her problems, but I wasn't ready on that day for a lot of heavy conversation. I conveniently finished my sandwich and suddenly realized I was late for an appointment. She gave me her phone number, but I never bothered to call."

As Tom's encounter shows, communication with those whom we have just met should not be too intimate. Too much personal disclosure too soon is threatening, not unlike taking off your clothing upon being introduced to someone. Discussing very personal information very early in the relationship seems to reduce our attractiveness to others. Although the exact reasons are unclear, it seems people are put off by others who reveal more about themselves than the current stage of a relationship appears to warrant. Moreover, prematurely discussing your very personal business appears to lower the probability that your prospective partners will later wish to reveal personal things about themselves; they probably no longer trust your judgment to handle such information discreetly. Unfortunately, because they are usually unaware of the implications of what they say, people who make these kinds of communication mistakes are inclined to do so repeatedly.

In short, while the sharing of intimate information tends to enhance our attraction to others, it seems best to take a "go slow" approach. Revealing too much of yourself too soon may frighten prospective partners away. Intimate disclosures between you and your partner should be mutual. That is, the first disclosures between you and your partner should be about equal in their level of intimacy: don't let these levels of intimacy become imbalanced.

If You Have An Early Disagreement

This book focuses on establishing new relationships rather than fixing old ones. However, even during our efforts to get a new relationship started, things don't always go quite as planned. What should you do if you have a disagreement at the very outset of a new relationship? Attempt to resolve the issue quickly. I am not suggesting that you give in to some ridiculous demand, or say you are sorry for something that is clearly the other person's fault. But I am saying that you should attempt to resolve the dispute or misunderstanding with all deliberate speed. Making up quickly is very important to the success of a new relationship. Because newly acquainted couples don't know what to expect from each other, a minor dispute has the potential to create considerable anxiety. What may be only a minor disagreement is likely to become more difficult to resolve with the passage of time. Besides not knowing what to expect of the other in the face of a confrontation, there are a number of factors that may contribute to the passage of time worsening the situation for both parties.

First, the longer a misunderstanding remains unresolved, the more time partners have to come up with reasons why each thinks the other is wrong. Mental replays of an altercation and the accompanying self-serving justifications only serve to harden both you and your partner's respective positions. Second, with the passage of time, each of you is likely to discuss the "disagreement" with a family member or friend who invariably will take each of your respective sides. Once your supporters begin to take sides, it becomes more difficult for the two of you to make up and somehow not appear to lose face. Thus each of you is less inclined to agree that it might have been a no-fault argument, or, God forbid, that one of you was wrong. If you need to take some time to let tempers or feelings cool down, then do so. But attempt to resolve the argument as soon as possible and move on! If such a disagreement is handled quickly and amicably, it may serve to strengthen your relationship by suggesting that the two of you are able to work through your differences.

Should You Play Hard To Get?

Should you string your suitors along for a while before accepting their advances, or should you seize what may be the magic moment? There are arguments for and against either strategy. Appearing to be too eager is probably unwise. As outlined in our earlier discussion on RMV, people like to believe that they are selecting romantic partners who are just as desirable (if not more) as themselves: that is, people of comparable RMV. If we are perceived as being too eager to date others, those who once perceived us as RMV equals may come to perceive us as having a lesser RMV, as evidenced by our "desperate" grab at what must be for us an exceptionally good deal. It does seem that people are often attracted to dating partners who are just beyond their reach, or for whose attention they have had to work hard. However, in many instances, it seems that most of us are attracted to those people who are hard for others to get, but not us! This belief probably enhances our self-esteem. Just playing hard to get, however, is probably not a good romantic strategy. Most of us do not handle repeated rejection very well!

But if you are bent on using a hard-to-get strategy, employ it sparingly. It would seem wise not to appear overly hard to get, especially to those whom you would actually like to be "gotten by." At the same time, some care must be taken so as to not appear to be overly eager to date those who seek to romance us, even when we're actually dying to romance them. So, when the likes of Denzel Washington or Olivia Brown drop by, let the door bell ring at least twice. Inform them that you're terribly busy, but because they're special, you will consider taking off from your busy schedule and agree to meet them for lunch—that is, if they can wait until after your 11:45 appointment.

Is There A Best Time To Ask For A Date?

There probably is, although it is bound to be different for each person. Psychologists have given some thought to the relationship between the timing of a dating request and the probability of its acceptance. Our intuition tells us that we should ask for a pay raise on a day when the boss is in a good mood. Asking someone out for a date may follow similar logic, but some research in this area of dating behavior suggests that the reverse might be true. It seems that individuals who have experienced at least a momentary loss of self-esteem may be more receptive to romantic advances than they might be otherwise. Persons experiencing a period of low self-esteem may at those times be in greater need of the affection of others and, subsequently, may be more likely to accept your romantic offer. However, you had better work fast, as they are likely to regain their sense of balance soon and put everything back into perspective—including you.

The GUE Method:
Beating The Midnight Hour

Before leaving our current discussion on timing and its effects on our romantic probabilities, I would like to share with you a story I heard while interacting with a group of black singles in their mid-to-late thirties. Included in the group was Johnetta, an attractive and highly sought-after woman, who told the story. I might add that the other men and women in the group had all heard of Johnetta's strategy, and attested to its validity. What she had to describe probably has never really been employed by anyone, least of all by pretty Johnetta. Yet, her comments did convey considerable insight into the relationship between timing and romantic opportunity.

Johnetta noted that the most attractive men she would see at night clubs, parties, and other social gatherings were the ones the women most actively pursued as romantic partners. As the evening wore on, these men were the first ones to become "unavailable." That meant only the least desirable dates were left during the waning hours of a particular social event. However, Johnetta says she soon realized that there was also fierce competition for these less attractive dates with the passage of time. Therefore, as a strategy to increase her chances of being "chosen," Johnetta says she began to employ the GUE method, GUE standing for "Going Ugly Early." She said that early in the evening, she would accept the advances of one of the men who was not among the most physically attractive of those present. That meant she found a partner, if not a handsome one, while the competition for him was lowest, and hence the probabilities of obtaining him highest.

Theoretically at least, the GUE method makes sense, given the dynamics of timing and competition. Undoubtedly, the viability of this approach would depend on how motivated a person is to obtain a date and, perhaps more importantly, how unattractive a date one is willing to accept at any given time in order to make the strategy work. In describing this strategy, Johnetta made the whole crowd break out in laughter. She later confessed that she only thinks of employing the GUE method after she has had too much to drink, and after most of the men have already been taken, including the "ugly" ones.

93

Dating With Children

When we were younger, most of us probably thought that by the time we had children we would no longer be seeking new romantic partners. Of course, for some individuals this is true. But increasing numbers of people are becoming single parents with children. Those of you who have children, or have dated people who do, know that children can have a significant effect on your dating activities. If you have children, your success in establishing and maintaining romantic relationships will depend on a variety of factors. Take, for example, the age of your children. As you know, very young children need a great deal of care; this may leave you less time to devote to your new partner. By the same token, older children may be less accepting of your dating behavior, and may view your partners as competitors for your time.

Also important is the type of relationship you have with your children. If you have a relatively closed relationship with your children and have included few individuals besides yourself in their lives, they may respond negatively to new people. However, if they are accustomed to sharing you with others, a new partner may arouse little concern. This issue, too, will vary in importance with the age of your children. Younger teenagers, for example, may be very protective of their time with you and may resist your spending time with a new partner. In contrast, older teenagers are apt to be doing their own thing, and may be glad to have you pay less attention to what they are doing.

Money is frequently another big issue for single parents who date. Kids usually consume a significant proportion of a single parent's resources. As a result, they may have little money to spend on dating activities. Potential partners who have children may understand this reality better than those who do not. By contrast, individuals without children who have typically dated others without children may feel required to contribute disproportionately toward the cost of the relationship. In an attempt to "make things fair" they can simply refuse to contribute more for dating activities than does the partner with children. A more common strategy is to engage in free or lower-cost dating activities.

If you are a single parent, should you date someone who doesn't have children? Of course, there is no single best answer to that question. Yet my personal experiences and discussions with single parents suggest that individuals who have children themselves make the best dating partners for singles with children. They seem to relate better to children, are more willing to engage in "family" activities with children, and are more understanding when children interfere with some previously planned activity. I believe that fellow singles with children offer the greatest probability of establishing and maintaining something other than perhaps a few sexual liaisons. It's important to realize that many people over twenty-five years old who do not have children have chosen to be childless. So do not be surprised if people whom you might like to date are not interested in becoming involved with your children. Whether you feel it's fair or not, many people who do not have children (and even some who do) are apt to feel inconvenienced by yours. In particular, they may not like the restrictions children often place on romantic relationships.

Of course, there are many successful dating couples where one partner has children and the other does not. So do not completely write off potential partners who do not have children. There are plenty of childless individuals out there who will happily accept your children as being part of the experience of dating you. They may have always wanted to have children but for some reason did not. Others may have never really thought much about having children, and may find dating you to be a unique opportunity to experience knowing children as well. Still others may just find your kids to be especially appealing.

Now for the reverse question: should you date someone who has children, if you don't? It depends. If you do, you must accept the fact that dating a person with kids will be more restrictive than dating someone who does not. It will affect what you can do, where you can do it, and how often. You must be willing to alter your conception of dating to include the children. It would also help if you like children in general, and your partner's children in particular. If you have responded positively to these ideas, then dating someone with children should pose few problems for you.

Your efforts to accept and get to know the children of those you date may, however, be rebuffed. Some single parents do not want their dates to become involved with their children, at least not initially.

95

Some single parents fear that by being introduced to their dates, their children may become confused as to who their "real" parents are. Still other single parents may attempt to prevent their children from establishing attachments with you for fear of disappointing the children if the relationship with you is short-lived. Therefore you may find, despite your ready acceptance of a partner's children, that in some instances it can take a long time before the parent feels comfortable having you around his or her children.

Thirtysomething And Still Single?

Why are there so many black singles in their late thirties and forties who are still dating? Has not the time passed for them to have found partners and settled down? Obviously not. Two primary factors contribute to this situation. First, as with white couples, these days both black men and black women are waiting longer to get married, or deciding not to marry at all. Secondly, because almost two out of three black marriages end in divorce, many blacks find themselves single again. Moreover, you are apt to notice more black women than black men who are in their thirties and forties and still single. This is so because the remarriage rate for black men is higher than that for black women, and because there are just more black women than black men in America.

Despite society's increasing tolerance for different lifestyles, being "thirtysomething," single, and never having married still has a certain stigma attached to it. This fact is especially true for women. Most males and females who remain single after the age of thirty report increasing pressure from family and friends to get married. People, especially older people, are inclined to begin asking what is wrong with someone who is in his or her late thirties and not yet married. The question most often asked is, "Is he or she homosexual?" Some may be, but the vast majority of never-married black singles are not. When asked why they have never married, they are likely to tell you that they have just not found what they are looking for, or have experienced a series of relationships that might have ended in marriage, but for whatever reason did not. Some have spent their time and energy focusing on their careers, or perhaps on the troubles of other family members. Others just enjoy being single and are not really trying to find a life-long partner. They have perhaps gotten used to doing their own thing, enjoying the social and economic flexibility being single affords them. Many people who have never married (and some who were once married) view the commitment of marriage to be inconsistent with their values and desired lifestyles.

There is a strong tendency in our society to criticize people who do not want to make lasting romantic commitments. But maybe we should criticize less those individuals who know and admit what they do not want. Instead, we might criticize more those who make romantic commitments that they then soon break, leaving behind broken hearts and broken families.

Does waiting longer to get married make it harder to do? This seems to be the case, at least for men. It appears that men become increasingly poor candidates for marriage after reaching forty years of age. Recent data suggests that the vast majority of men who have never married by the age of forty never will. Because many forty-year-old men have lived alone, they often know how to "take care" of themselves. They may, therefore, be less in need of someone to take care of them, and more in need of someone to do things with. So, if your goal in dating is to get married, then your probabilities of doing so are better if you date someone who is under forty, or who has been previously married. However, if your goal in seeking romantic partners is not necessarily marriage, but instead companionship, age is a less important consideration.

8 Perceiving Fairness, Experiencing Happiness

"It's good to find someone that you can go down the middle of the road with . . ."

These words from the song "50-50 Love," performed by Teddy Pendergrass, may well contain the secret to maintaining a successful romantic relationship. Your ability as a couple to establish a 50-50 love, and what I shall call fairness, significantly influences your feelings about your relationship. Despite the temptations to get as much as you can from a partner, the evidence shows that you are likely to be happiest when you feel that both what you get and what you give in a relationship are equal to what your partner gets and gives.

Even in the very early phases of romance, experiencing a sense of mutual fairness may be the most important factor in determining whether your new relationship will work. Fairness tends to make for more intimate, satisfying, and stable relationships. And those of you for whom sex is important will be happy to know that relationships that couples view as fair are apt to be more sexually satisfying.

What do I mean by fairness? Fairness means partners feel they are receiving benefits from a relationship that are equal to their contributions. Whether you actually get as much out of a relationship as you put in, however, is not as important as whether you *feel* you're getting a fair deal. In short, your feelings about the fairness of the relationship are most important.

Let me explain this in more detail through some examples. First consider the experiences of John and Jackie, a couple involved in a relationship that's made for the 1990s. The first born in a family of four sons, John is the only son who did not attend college, and the only one who is married. But he has managed to do well economically with a busy foreign-car repair shop. Jackie, meanwhile, has turned the beauty shop business upside down using strong marketing tools she picked up from John. He told me in a teasing tone, "She's becoming a second Madam C. J. Walker." Among other things, her shop is open until midnight, and she caters mainly to busy professional women. I arranged a meeting with this couple after hearing them discuss their relationship on a call-in radio talk show. They invited me over one Sunday afternoon.

I was greeted at the door by the fragrance of fresh flowers, and by Jackie's reassuring smile. She has a round face, framed by closely cropped brown hair that blended nicely with her pecan-colored complexion. John, meanwhile, came from the back of the house, wearing a barbecue-spattered apron and announcing in a baritone voice that I was just in time to taste some of the best barbecue in this city.

"No," Jackie playfully corrected him, "in this country." "Maybe," I added, "in the world." We all laughed, and I followed them to their redwood patio. In no time, I realized that John had not been kidding. As I washed down the appetizing meal with iced tea, I was captivated by their landscaped backyard. On their carpet-like green lawn they had artfully placed wooden boxes holding a profusion of flowers—tulips and Dutch irises, roses and hyacinths, daffodils and crocuses. "That garden gets as much love and care as we give one another," Jackie said proudly. "We call it our joint venture."

I was struck by the warmth this couple exuded the entire time I was there. Throughout the afternoon, each occasionally touched the other gently while making a point, and both acted all the while as if they felt they were the luckiest couple in the world. "You may think we're putting on a show," John said, as if reading my mind. "I know what you're probably thinking. You're thinking that we're acting like we're the happiest couple in the world. Well, we are." Jackie reached over and pressed his hand gently, then got up to remove the dishes. "Some people ask us what's our secret," John said, his voice deeper now. "Hey, man, there ain't no secret, unless it's being in harmony. Sharing and fairness. I'm convinced those are the most important ingredients in a wholesome relationship."

His point about sharing I immediately understood. But fairness? That word stood out in my mind like block letters on a billboard, mainly because it jibed with much of what I had already read on the topic. I wanted to hear more, however; for instance, how can a man who earns so much more than his mate consider their relationship fair? John poured himself more tea, then moved his glass about and watched the ice cubes twirl with the motion. "I'm moving the glass in one direction and the ice cubes follow the motion. That's the way Jackie and I move in our relationship. We are in rhythm; we understand one another's needs. If we tried to move in the opposite direction of the natural flow of things, we'd create unnecessary tension and ruin the rhythm. I know it sounds simplistic." He smiled. "You say you caught us on the radio. Remember that loud brother who called in and sort of ridiculed us? He got pretty hot, didn't he? But as I said on the radio, I'm convinced that finding someone who is in rhythm with you is far more important than finding someone who has everything *except* that rhythm."

I had to steer him back to my initial question: what did that have to do with fairness? He then looked toward the sliding door leading to the kitchen, and seeing that Jackie was out of earshot, he continued to talk. "One day when I was down in Atlanta, I had lunch with an old high school buddy. Anyway, I told him about my marriage and my lady. Know what he said? He said, 'Man, how did you end up with a beautician? With your money, you can do a lot better.' I wanted to smack him. He was talking about my woman. But I kept my cool, sort of, explaining that if he ever met Jackie, he'd see why."

"Well, last Thanksgiving, the brother was supposed to bring his lady up to spend the weekend with us. He called a few days before the trip with a sad story. They'd busted up. She'd taken everything, except his underwear. I expressed my regrets." John then got to the heart of the matter. "I make good money, but I don't let money go to my head, if you know what I mean. Jackie doesn't have to work, but she insists on keeping her beauty business, partly because she wants to feel she's contributing to this relationship on every level. She pays for dinner as often as I do. Here's the compromise: when she pays, she treats me to meals that cost considerably less than where I'd take her.

"Sure, we eat at places like Red Lobster on evenings when Jackie picks up the tab, but I still feel I'm treated fairly because both of us contribute what we can to the cost of our nights on the town. But more important, we both contribute to one another's peace of mind."

John's attitude shows how a relationship might be perceived as fair even if contributions by the partners are not precisely equal. To be sure, couples contribute things other than money to their relationships. For example, you may give your partner more emotional support, and your partner may supply you with such things as prestige, status, or excitement, depending on what you need and value. Or, in return for your greater emotional support, you may receive help with housework, or in managing your financial affairs. This kind of fairness is typical of what happened in the relationship of a fashionable Cleveland couple, Jerry and Connie. Connie, who operates a bookkeeping service out of her home, says she used to dread the time when Jerry dropped by from his advertising copywriter job.

"If something went wrong at the office, I could tell as much from the time he'd set foot in the door," Connie recalled. "It would ruin our whole evening. He's usually talkative and very good company to me, but not when he's facing a tough deadline or when it appears the company is about to lose an account. I don't know that much about advertising, but I can imagine how emotionally draining it must be to try to come up with eye-catching material to sell products. I'll never forget the time when his agency went through what they called restructuring. That turned out to be a fancy way of saying lots of people were going to be let go. They didn't say who would get the axe for a month, and being around Jerry during those thirty days was misery piled upon misery.

"Luckily, he was one of the few blacks that the company didn't put on what they called 'indefinite furlough.' But right after that crisis, he and I sat down and had a heart-to-heart talk. We knew we loved one another very much, but his high-pressure job was ruining our relationship. I cried a lot before we had that talk, but one day it occurred to me that even though my work doesn't bring in nearly as much income as Jerry's, it doesn't cause me as much mental strain either." She paused. "I decided right then and there that maybe I could give him a lift whenever he needs to unwind. Just being there to listen to his woes has made a big difference. I can't match him in income, but I can be a good partner. We have no debate about who pays for our evenings out. Jerry pays. But we both see ourselves as providing something useful to the relationship. My emotional support balances out his financial support. We see that as fair, because this sort of give-and-take has helped us to establish a very good and stable relationship."

Because the types of contributions people make in relationships vary widely, it may take a greater number of one type to equal that of another. But the bottom line is that you must feel that what you receive is equal in value to what you are giving.

Nor are all of your contributions to your relationship exchanged in the same place, time, or manner. That is, there may not be an immediate tit for tat. For example, you may throw your partner a big, splashy birthday party. But your partner may honor you in a less conspicuous manner with a gift that satisfies an intimate, personal interest of yours. He or she may give you a special jazz tape, or surprise you with a set of Toni Morrison novels, or tickets to one of August Wilson's great plays. Or your partner could just as easily choose to take you on a relaxing weekend trip. In any case, the differences in the type, quality, and timing of such contributions sometimes make it difficult for outsiders to observe the fairness of your relationship.

This is why a stable and satisfactory relationship of ours may sometimes appear to be inequitable and unfair to our friends and family. Again, fairness is the feeling that you are receiving as much as you feel you deserve, even when your rewards may differ from what outsiders expect. This is especially true when considering qualities of an emotional nature, such as caring and support. But the principle remains the same—there must be a sense of fairness.

Understanding the dynamics of fairness is, I believe, crucial for black couples, because they so often are faced with situations that are unconventional in terms of the mainstream white society. For example, because black men so often face uncertain employment and professional futures, couples may rotate in their roles of providing the primary financial support for the relationship. This places black couples at odds with the traditional social expectation that males should always take major financial responsibility for relationships. Thus, when a black woman earns more than her partner, it has the potential to create tension for the couple. Warning—this expectation about men has outlived its time and usefulness and is now clearly dysfunctional for black couples! Changes in the employment opportunities available for black males and black females, even more so than for whites, require that black couples contribute to their relationships what they can, and ignore gender expectations as to who should contribute what.

Don't permit outmoded societal notions to dictate the reality of your unique situations. Society may say men should pay the bills, but what if you're a woman and your partner earns less than you do, and lacks the financial wherewithal to do all the things you want to do? Does that mean you should call it quits? Take the case of Denise. A single-parent who grew up in public housing, Denise might have become dependent on welfare, except for a take-charge attitude that made her strive for something better.

"I owe my independence to my grandmother," she said. "She's the reason I got through college. She kept my baby while I struggled with the books. It took me five years to finish, but I did it. I got a degree in business and found myself a job as a marketing saleswoman for a radio station. You wouldn't believe how many times I was interviewed and written about when I was eventually promoted to sales manager. I had mixed feelings about the attention, because the people doing the interviewing acted like black single parents from the projects weren't *supposed* achieve."

By the time Denise reached the top in her department, she was earning more than enough money to pay her own way. Here began her dilemma. She had never dated anyone who had offered to pay the cost of dating until she met Warren, an insurance salesman.

When they first began dating, Denise readily accepted Warren's setting the social standard by paying for most of the entertainment, although she always paid for her own baby-sitter. Then came a sorority dance to benefit the victims of hunger in Ethiopia. This dance called for formal dress. Warren didn't own a tuxedo, so he would have to rent one. Tickets, moreover, were $150 per couple. Denise didn't know at the time that Warren had to choose between paying his car note and attending this function. He chose the car. Instead of telling her the truth, he simply canceled the date at the last minute.

"I fumed when he told me he was passing up the one Christmas holiday social event that I wanted to attend. Problem number one: I never thought about Warren's financial circumstances. I felt really awful when he told me the real reason he cancelled the date. Problem number two: I liked Warren's company much better than I liked being with a lot of other men.

"We decided it was time to drop the pretensions, and we made a list of priorities. We agreed that his salary wasn't enough to handle all of my social demands. So it was only fair for me to chip in. I now pay for most of the cost of dating—especially the big events. I like being with him just that much, and I like him even more now that he's getting away from his hang-ups about what a man's role should be."

Both Warren and Denise perceive this new arrangement as being fair, and they are able to go out more frequently. They could of course have chosen to attend fewer activities, or Denise could have found someone who offered her more financially. In that sense, Denise saw her decision to share the cost as being especially fair in relation to the enjoyment she feels in being with Warren.

Black women like Denise who earn more than their partners, should accept the fact that they might have to shoulder more of the financial responsibility if doing so proves acceptable to both partners. Instead of clinging to the notion that the male should pay for everything, or should pay more, these women and their partners should attempt to find a way to make their relationships fair. This, I believe, is best done by changing their notions of the way things are supposed to be, and thus what constitutes fairness. Needless to say, the more equal you and your partner are in your abilities to give each other financial and emotional support, the easier it will be to establish a perception of fairness in your relationship.

Beware Of The Greedy

There are some partners who expect to contribute virtually nothing to a relationship, and they may also have unfair expectations of what they should receive. We typically call these people "gold diggers." They expect that their romantic partners will give them more than they are willing to give others. Typically, they are freeloaders. Consider Elaine, who dresses as if she's always in the *Ebony* Fashion Fair. Her male counterpart is another acquaintance of mine named Robert, whose ego stays on Cloud Nine because women constantly tell him he bears a resemblance to Billy Dee Williams. Though I know these two just casually, I have observed them in enough settings to know that they both must have received a great deal of indulgence at some point in their lives. This shows in the way they treat—and lose—partners. Robert acts as if he's entitled to gifts from women—including their credit cards—and Elaine's motto seems to be that it is always better to receive than to give.

As children, people like Elaine and Robert might have been especially attractive or talented, and thus received a large amount of their families' resources, time, and attention. Perhaps their parents taught them to expect great returns from others, but forgot to teach their children about the other side of the coin—that this would require them to give a great deal themselves. On the other hand, it is quite possible that people like Elaine and Robert have had very hard lives, and have decided to exploit others whenever possible. In either case, they have come to expect unfair returns in their relationships. They expect to receive the lion's share of attention and resources.

Individuals who come to expect, if not demand, more from their partners than they are willing to give are typically faced with one of two options. They will have to move in and out of short-term romantic relationships, breaking them off as their partners begin to demand a fairer return on their own romantic contributions. Or else they must be willing to date individuals who are clearly less desirable than themselves, people with conspicuously lower RMV. This is usually someone who is willing, as compensation for their lesser desirability, to "over benefit" or "sugar daddy" (or "sugar mama") their romantic partners.

The drawbacks of the first strategy are obvious, in that these individuals are destined to engage in a series of short-term relationships that will often end unpleasantly. The latter strategy, that of dating partners with lower RMVs than themselves, may also have unpleasant consequences. It is my guess, however, that dating less desirable partners is the more common strategy of those who are truly determined to give less in their relationships. Despite receiving windfall returns on their meager romantic investments, the exploiters are unlikely to enjoy the company of those whom they exploit. Moreover, the "less desirable" romantic partner may at some point decide simply to stop giving more.

In brief, stay away from these truly greedy types! They have yet to learn that fairness is the key to sustaining romance.

How And Why Relationships Become Unfair

There are two chief reasons why you may begin to see a relationship as unfair: first, if there is an *actual* change in your contributions or those of your partner; second, if one of you *perceives* a change in the value or importance of your individual contributions. Let's consider the former situation first.

The traditional marriage vows are a good example of society's attempt to encourage couples to remain in their relationships, even if their abilities to provide for each other should change. For example, the statements "for richer or poorer, better or worse," are in effect asking the couple to agree to stay together even if their circumstances change. Even though dating singles don't take vows, they do have some basic expectations regarding continued fairness in their relationships. Jerome, a young graduate of an East Coast medical school, had been dating Donna, a school social worker, since his first year of residency. However, when Jerome finished his residency, what had been a beautiful romance began to experience difficulties. What before had been a fair relationship, based on their respective abilities to contribute to it, came to be seen as an unfair relationship. Jerome, now a full-fledged doctor, commanded considerably more professional prestige and earned considerably more money than Donna. He told her, "Everyone else now gives me more attention and respect, and I like it." As a consequence Jerome felt that since he now had more to bring to the relationship—that is, more money and prestige—he could also expect to receive more from Donna in the way of her contributions.

Donna, on the other hand, said, "Since Jerome has become a 'god'

—excuse me, I mean a doctor—he expects me to show him greater respect and deference, and give him more attention, with no similar increase in the amount of respect and attention he shows me. He even expects to do fewer of his share of unpleasant tasks such as the dishes." After a few months of what she perceived to be the growing unfairness in their relationship, Donna decided to call it quits. They made up, however, and sought counseling in order to work through their crisis. Actually, the situation with Jerome and Donna is not that uncommon. They were fortunate in that they cared enough about each other to seek counseling and obtain insight into what had gone awry in their relationship, and to work to correct it.

Similar dynamics may be at work when someone attempts to sabotage the efforts of a partner to enhance himself or herself in some way. Joining a weight-loss program or engaging in some form of professional improvement are good examples. If, for instance, you are overweight and are making efforts to lose some pounds, there is a good chance that this would improve your level of attractiveness. If you view being attractive as a resource that you contribute to your relationships (and it most surely is), then enhancing your level of attractiveness also increases your contribution to your relationship. But, if you contribute more to a relationship, you may come to expect to receive more in return. Your partner in turn may feel pressured to increase his or her contributions in some way, so as to once again make the relationship equitable or fair. Or your partner might resort to sabotage. That is, he or she may attempt to prevent you from increasing your contributions to the relationship—so as not to feel compelled to increase his or her own contributions.

This is rather common in the case of upwardly mobile black couples, where one partner's attempt at self-improvement is sometimes viewed as a threat by the other. Take the case where a woman decides to go back to school to obtain a bachelor's degree. Ordinarily, this might be viewed as a step toward reaching better-paying jobs and a means to bring more financial resources to a relationship. On the other hand, it can be perceived as threatening, especially if that woman's partner thinks this change in economic status will mean that more will be expected of him. Instead of helping her get the degree, the threatened partner may work against this effort, whether subtly or overtly.

Any efforts by one partner to enhance himself or herself can have the effect of changing the perceived degree of fairness in the relationship. Indeed, any actual self-improvement on the part of one partner may either seem threatening to the other partner, or may motivate that partner to improve as well, in order to keep the relationship fair. Hence, it may be a misguided effort to retain their relationship's existing fairness that prompts some individuals to try to prevent their partners from engaging in self-improvement.

The second most common way that a relationship can move from a fair state to an unfair one is for one or both of the partners to change their perceptions of the value, or importance, of their contributions to the relationship. For example, a heightened sense of your own value may lead you to view your contributions as being more valuable than your partner's. This may result from some significant life event that has enhanced your sense of self-esteem. Or indeed, you may simply feel that the existing situation has been unfair all the time, but that you just hadn't been aware of it; now, perhaps, you are deciding that you're "not going to take it anymore." In either case, the key is that there has not been a change in the actual contributions to the relationship. Rather, you or your partner have merely reevaluated the worth of your personal contributions. This change results in the perception that the relationship is unfair—and creates problems.

Are You Giving Until It Hurts?

Closely related to those who don't give enough are those who give too much in their romantic relationships. They're like Deena, a twenty-eight-year-old school teacher who finds it difficult to sustain romantic relationships in spite of her beauty and poise. She is kind-hearted and enjoys giving; often, in fact she gives expensive gifts to her dates. Her problem is that her gifts serve to confuse her partners. Some think they are expected to give gifts in return, even if they don't want to. Some even think she's trying to "buy" them, and become resentful. Deena came to me to discuss her problem. She played the role of the victim, saying the men she was attracted to were unappreciative. It was only after much discussion that she revealed with some embarrassment her habit of showering men with expensive gifts. She finally asked the right question: Did I think that perhaps these gifts were harming her relationships?

It's definitely possible for a relationship to be harmed by one partner's *receiving* more than he or she feels is fair. As I've said, there exists considerable research to support the fact that both men and women are more content, happy, and sexually satisfied in relationships they perceive as fair. Getting too much, like not getting enough, can be damaging to relationships. Although partners who receive too much from a relationship may be delighted with the things they get, they also are likely to experience feelings of guilt, and perhaps feelings of being obligated or entrapped.

Over-giving also has the potential to cause our partners to question our romantic desirability. They are probably aware that the giving of more than one's fair share is often a way in which a partner attempts to compensate for his or her lower RMV. Such compensation may consist of providing the more desirable partner with "extras," which may be any kind of benefit like gifts or favors. While perhaps enjoying these unanticipated benefits, those who receive them may feel uncomfortable. They may also begin to question why they are being treated so well. In fact, excessive compliments (even when true) may have a similar negative effect.

In other words, when romantic partners feel they are getting more than what's fair, they may misconstrue our motives, just as those who are too generous may misinterpret our reactions to their extreme generosity. This situation creates misunderstandings on the parts of both those who receive too much and those who give too much. We have all heard the expression that someone was "too nice," just as we may have heard someone describe a partner as "mistaking my kindness for weakness."

I do not wish to put down gift-giving or suggest that couples should not be thoughtful, as can be expressed in the offering of small gifts such as cologne, flowers, or dinner. However, giving gifts or providing other goodies that are clearly beyond the expectations of either partner (or anyone else for that matter) may cause recipients to question the genuineness of the giver's attraction. So restraining your giving to a reasonable level is apt to help maintain a relationship your partner will perceive as fair.

Why Do We Remain In Unfair Relationships?

Despite your desire to be in fair relationships, you may at times have found yourself in unfair ones. Fortunately, many unfair relationships are short-lived; however, some are not. Most of us have at one time or another remained in some relationship despite the fact that we felt it was unfair. Why? Of course there are innumerable possibilities, but there are at least four basic situations that are likely to contribute to your remaining in an unfair relationship. Let's review them.

I have already partly outlined one situation, in the discussion of gold diggers. As I noted, romantic partners are most likely to have a mate of equal romantic desirability. But when one partner is less so, that partner may try to compensate by giving the other more than he or she should get. Such a strategy, although inherently unfair, is not that uncommon; but it rarely makes for successful relationships. It seems gold digger-types stay in unfair romantic relationships because they like the extra rewards or goodies they receive. Over-givers, on the other hand, may be slow to break off such a relationship because they think it allows them to hold on to a partner they otherwise wouldn't be able to keep. But these scenarios are unlikely to result in long-term happiness. Ultimately, one or both parties will seek to correct what they perceive as an unfair situation.

A second reason why you may remain in an unfair relationship is the lack of an alternative. In this situation you perceive yourself as trapped between what you feel you deserve on one hand, and what the romantic marketplace has to offer on the other. In other words, you may be receiving less from your romantic partner than you feel you deserve or, at any rate, less than you have come to expect. However, you may not view yourself as having any options that are better (or maybe even as good) as your current relationship.

Take the example of Bernard. At thirty-five years old, Bernard prides himself on his physique, but one of his main assets—to women, at least—is his income. He isn't exactly handsome, but he earns a good salary as a pipe fitter. The woman in his life is twenty-year-old Linda, whose tastes lean toward cornrow hairstyles and colorful African garments. Linda, too, makes a good income as a real estate agent. In order to earn her pay, however, Linda has to work most weekends and many evenings.

"That's what irritates me most about our relationship," Bernard said. "Unless I cook myself, I end up eating alone, mostly at soul food restaurants. Linda, you see, seldom cooks. Selling houses is a trip. I'm lucky if we eat together once a week. Linda's work does not permit her to spend much time baking pies and being a homebody." Nevertheless, Bernard thinks he should have a partner who makes him dinner and is a good homemaker. He believes he can find other women who are better at meeting his domestic needs, but not one as physically attractive as Linda. So, for the time being, he'll continue to date Linda while looking for a partner who better satisfies his needs.

Similarly, Linda feels Bernard is not as sensitive or as good looking as she would like her mate to be. But she believes that guys whom she finds better looking and more sensitive lack Bernard's potential to provide for the family she would like to have. Hence she, too, will stay in the relationship for the time being, but she'll keep an eye out for a better catch.

This situation points to another important fact: although you may seek fairness, you also are likely to consider your options upon ending an unfair relationship. This reinforces the point that the extent to which you are willing to tolerate an unfair relationship is partly a function of romantic marketplace conditions—i.e. available suitors—and not an indication of your appetite for abuse, as some of your relatives or close friends may suggest. Ironically, those who have the most to give are apt to have the most difficult time finding partners of equal RMV. Hence, their lower chances for finding suitable partners may lead them to stay in unfair relationships longer. This is likely to result in their going for longer time periods between romantic partners once they leave unfair relationships.

A third situation in which some people may elect to remain in unfair relationships is when they are receiving those things from their partners that are most important to them. Not all of your needs are of equal importance: some are clearly more important to you than others. Thus you may view your overall relationship to be unfair, and yet remain in the relationship because it provides you with important benefits—such as security, affection, money, or even sex.

Stan and Veronica, for instance, had been dating for two years. A musician, Stan dresses as if he is still living in the be-bop era. He sports a goatee and wears silk scarves instead of neckties when his all-black trio performs at hotels and restaurants in the Memphis area. Stan comes in contact with a variety of people and he's naturally gregarious on and off the bandstand. Unlike Stan, Veronica is as reserved in social settings as she is with the math students she teach at a Memphis high school—which is why Stan feels Veronica is too much of a wallflower. However, Stan stayed in the relationship because Veronica, more so than any woman he had ever dated, satisfied him sexually. And for Stan, a good sexual relationship has always ranked high on his list of romantic priorities. To use his expression, "Love don't mean a thing if it ain't got that zing."

At the same time, Veronica is unhappy with Stan's inability to manage money. Yet despite Stan's financial ineptitude, he always treated Veronica with respect and courtesy, behavior she found more satisfying than being with a man who may drive a BMW or have a professional title, but has no respect for her feelings or psychological needs. Given the importance of sex to Stan and respect to Veronica, these two are likely to continue to date. Indeed, their relationship is likely to sustain itself for as long as the major determinants for their happiness are being met, despite their more general level of dissatisfaction.

Finally, we may elect to remain in an unfair relationship because we perceive the consequences of leaving the relationship to be too high. I'm thinking here of Jeff and Alice, both of whom came from prominent old black families with money. They have been dating since they met in college in Atlanta and have at times been tagged as one of their community's leading black couples. Furthermore, their families have even become friends during the course of their romance. However, in the past year they have been in and out of love with each other. Now they find themselves more out than in, and yet the thought of calling off their romantic relationship is unpleasant and awkward for them both.

Like Jeff and Alice, we may not wish to experience or cause others the emotional pain that sometimes accompanies the breaking off of a relationship. Or we may not wish to face the reactions of family and friends to our break-up. We may feel that a break-up will be a source of embarrassment or shame. We may also be concerned that others will view our break-up as an inability on our part to form lasting relationships (which is a possibility). Or we may simply not wish to go through the hassles of attempting to find a new romantic partner.

Despite the fact that we may be receiving an insufficient return on our contributions to a given relationship, there may be some aspect of the relationship that we hate to give up—even if it is *not* something we are most looking for in a partner—and hence we maintain our involvement despite our overall dissatisfaction. For example, you may enjoy having access to some things, e.g. your partner may get tickets to all the black plays and concerts that come to town. Or we may not wish to lose the status or prestige of being associated with dating a particular person. Of course, it could be said that in such instances we may be electing to remain in a relationship for what seem to be "all the wrong reasons." We may find ourselves staying in unfair relationships because we hate to experience a loss, or admit we've made a mistake. While there are surely other reasons why many of us have remained in relationships we felt were unfair, I have attempted to capture some of the major ones. Also, it is likely that our past reasons for remaining in "unfair" relationships have been a function of more than one—if not all—of the above mentioned reasons.

In your efforts to address what you perceive to be your own unfair relationships, I believe you must do one of two things. First, you can finally "just say no," that you're not willing to accept your current situation anymore—which is likely to give you more time to look for a "fairer" one. Or second, you may want to adjust your judgment about how unfair your current relationship really is. For example, a good romantic deal is at least in part determined by what is available at the time—sort of like interest rates. That is, you may need to assess your perception of what is good in light of romantic marketplace conditions, e.g. the quality of other available partners. You may need to reevaluate what you have in the way of a partner given what is available, rather than what you would most like. You may find that your current partner, given the going market, is pretty good after all.

Is Money The Most Important Thing? No, But...

The issue of money is especially important to black couples because they so often have too little of it. Money is virtually always an important issue for couples. Unless you and your partner can reach some agreement on how to address the issue of what is financially fair, your relationship is likely to be short-lived. It is not the absolute number of dollars that's important, but rather the feelings you and your partner have about the financial state of the relationship. With respect to many dating couples, "I don't have any money" is probably a more frequent comment than the truth: "Why should I pay?"

Most often the heart of such disputes involves the issue of fairness. There are, however, a number of advantages to both partners contributing equitably to the cost of their dating activities. First, people who offer to pay their share are viewed very differently than those who do not. Offering to pay suggests that you have at least some money, which is always a good sign. Few of us want a person who doesn't have at least some financial resources. Second, it suggests that you aren't asking to be cared for, and in this way you show some sense of your own independence. Third, at least offering to contribute financially eliminates the implicit assumption that you are saying, "In order to get to know me you have to pay for it." Fourth, it says that when the date is over, neither party is indebted to, or owes, the other anything. Fifth, neither party is likely to feel exploited or unfairly treated, a negative feeling that is especially likely if the partners have comparable incomes and resources. Finally, a sense of respect is more likely to result between you and your partner when you view each other as being fair.

The major point here is not how much any given partner should pay, but rather that dating singles should feel that their partner is making a fair contribution to the relationship. Most people who can afford to pay don't mind doing so, as long as they view their partner as being willing to contribute something.

A final word on the issue of money. Money can be a great source of power in dating relationships. It has a tremendous potential to make otherwise fair relationships unfair. Because their incomes are often similar, black males and black females, more so than white couples, may be at risk of perceiving each other as being economically unfair in terms of traditional gender-role expectations. If current black educational and employment trends prevail, an increasing number of black women will make more money than do many of the men they might like to date. Changes in the potential earning power of black males and females, in conjunction with the uncertain employment picture for black males, suggest that black couples will need to exercise increasing sensitivity toward each other on the issue of money. Most importantly, black couples must perceive their partners to be contributing their fair share in their relationships. They must come to realize that the absolute amount of money that each partner spends is not so important as whether their partners feel themselves to be treated fairly.

9 Bases of Romantic Power

WHENEVER PEOPLE TALK about Alice Walker's book *The Color Purple*, they naturally get around to the character of "Mister," the abusive husband, one of the most despicable characters in African-American literature. Although he is unlikable in every respect, Mister exemplifies in the extreme the human drive for power in relationships. In spite of his crudeness and cruelty, however, Mister is no different from many people in real life, where the instinct to have control is played out in a more sophisticated fashion in almost all human endeavors—in church and on the dance floor, in the board room and in the bedroom. Fortunately, most black men and women who are successful in exercising power or influence in relationships are far cries from Mister. They are not bullies; they are more subtle, diplomatic even, in asserting themselves. Above all, they are far more sensitive to the needs of their partners.

Power, in the context of relationships, means having the ability to influence your partner. You possess power to the extent that you are able to get your romantic partners to do those things you want them to do. Power as an issue in romantic relationships is important because you must frequently look to your partner to meet many of your most basic needs. The more power you have, the more likely you are to have those needs satisfied.

Blacks, like other people, often experience considerable difficulty understanding and using power in their romantic relationships. More-over, the power dynamics of black couples tend to differ from those of white couples, as I mentioned briefly in the Introduction.

First, black men tend to have greater power than their partners at the beginning of a romantic relationship. As we have noted, there are fewer eligible black men than there are black women (and this ratio is less dramatic for whites). This situation increases the leverage of black men in the romantic marketplace, since they are in shorter supply and have a wider selection of potential partners to choose from.

Black females however, unlike white females, are often able to exert more power during the later course of the relationship. This is so because black females have incomes and professional statuses similar to those of their partners; hence, they are able to call more shots, so to speak, than their white female counterparts. These two factors—a significant gender imbalance that favors black men, and approximately equal levels of financial and professional statuses between black men and women—contribute most to the unique power dynamics of black couples.

Knowing The Needs Of Your Partner

My goal in this chapter is to enhance the power of those partners who lack it, and to tame the use of power by those who abuse it. The extent of your power and influence in your relationships is most affected by three factors. The first is the needs of your romantic partners; the second is the extent to which you are willing or able to satisfy those needs; and the third is the availability of romantic alternatives.

By knowing the needs of your partner, you enhance your ability to influence him or her. Your partner may need any number of things: companionship, sex, love, security, status, money. Indeed, the greater the needs of your partner, and the more capable you are of satisfying them, the more influence you are able to exert in your relationship. A first step toward gaining power, then, is to assess the needs of your partner. Chances are that you unconsciously made such an assessment at the start of your relationship. The list below is typical of the desires those in search of romantic partners frequently express:

Men's Desires	Women's Desires
1. Good looks	1. Honesty
2. Sex	2. Wealth
3. Charm	3. Good looks
4. Maturity	4. Sex

Of course, the expressed needs or desires of your partner may differ from those cited above. One of the best ways to assess your potential partner's needs is to ask about the attributes of his or her former partners. Such a discussion (which some might find difficult) should give you an idea of what the person is looking for in a romantic partner.

Black men and women tend to have most of the same wants in a relationship; however, as the above list shows, their order of priorities may be different. In any case, most people have a number of needs that they perceive to be critical, and that they consistently attempt to satisfy. These are their "must" items. Review the general desires listed above and determine whether any of them fits your own partner's needs. If so, jot them down. Add to the list the needs and wants that your partner mentioned when the two of you discussed the subject. Then try to make some assessment as to your ability or willingness to satisfy them.

If you consistently find yourself having too little power in your romantic relationships, it is most likely a consequence of three factors: either you have selected partners whose needs you do not meet, partners to whom you have too little to offer, or partners who command too much power in the romantic marketplace.

Realizing What You Have To Offer

After determining the needs of your partner, you must then decide whether you are able or willing to satisfy those needs. For example, if your partner craves really wild, kinky sex, and you doubt your ability to deliver, then you are unlikely to have much power in the relationship. Remember that your romantic partners are only likely to let you exert influence in their lives to the extent that you are offering them things they value and enjoy.

The Availability Of Options

Ask yourself these crucial questions: How easy would it be for your partner to replace you? Are there lots of romantically desirable individuals whom he or she could find to take your place? The value of a romantic partner, like the value of most things, is in part determined by availability.

This point brings to mind Janet, a beautician in her mid-thirties from Winston-Salem, North Carolina. Whenever I saw her, all of her conversation would center around her boyfriend at the time, Steven, a car salesman. I never had the opportunity to meet him, but I was a friend of one of Janet's customers, Bettye, who expressed more than a little concern about the relationship. "Personally, I wouldn't give Steven the dust off my floor," Bettye said, "but I'm polite to him for Janet's sake. All she talks about is Steven this and Steven that, yet we all know he isn't worth the trouble. He throws the whole shop in disarray soon as he walks through the front door. We might be sitting around catching up on the latest gossip. Then here he comes, clean as a black banker with holes in his pockets. Usually he'll hit on Janet for money, which all of us know he has no intention of repaying. He seldom takes her out and, to make matters worse, he openly flirts with the customers. Like I say, we're nice to him because we don't want to hurt her feelings, but one Friday night we got up enough courage to ask her why she tolerates Steven's crazy behavior. She made up a lot of excuses for him, but what it boiled down to was that Janet didn't feel she could find anybody else."

What Bettye and the other customers probably didn't realize was that Janet had found herself in the same boat as many other sisters. Because there are significantly more eligible black females than black males, average-looking women like Janet are often at a disadvantage in the romantic marketplace. Since these women have fewer romantic choices, they often experience less power in their romantic relationships. They are unquestionably in a tight market, competing for a scarce number of eligible black men.

In contrast, most heterosexual black men who are drug-free and employed have a variety of attractive black women to chose from. All things considered, the fewer potential romantic options you have, the weaker your base of power. The gross imbalance of black females to males explains why cities such as Washington have reputations for being good romantic marketplaces for black men and not so good for black women. However, it is often rumored that Washington's frequently noted gender imbalance is in fact propaganda put out by female Washingtonians in order to lure more black men to the city.

Yet there must be some truth to the gender imbalance issue in Washington, given the number of romantic horror stories that black women tell about the outlandish things black men get away with in the nation's capital. If the stories are true, it means that the brothers have so many romantic options that they can afford to abuse their power, and thus risk alienating a potential partner. It is for this reason also that black men are sometimes called "spoiled," a characterization that unfortunately is often generally applied to all black men.

Black women need not be overwhelmed by the gender imbalance, however. There are ways to remain powerful within a romantic relationship even if the numbers are against you. The trick is to have romantic resources that potential partners value. These resources enhance your attractiveness. By romantic resources, I mean those assets that can be used to benefit your partners and at the same time enhance your power within the relationship. Having lots of resources, however, is not so important as having the *right* resources. Let's take a brief look at some of these resources.

Love And Emotional Support

Affection, love, and understanding are extremely important attributes. Here, I think about Deborah. Slight and fine-featured, she has dark brown hair and chestnut-colored skin. She is the first to admit that John, a guy she frequently dates, isn't exceptionally attractive. But he is so loving and caring that Deborah finds herself always seeking out his company. Even when she has offers to go on dates with guys who are more physically appealing, she'll turn them down in order to spend time with John.

Like other resources, the ability to be warm and expressive toward others will not be evenly distributed among those you meet. Most of us are painfully aware of the wide disparity in the abilities of our partners to respond positively to us emotionally. Such differences were perhaps most notable in that some of your prior partners were better at providing support than others.

This works both ways; your capacity to give emotionally to others is apt to increase both your level of attractiveness and your partner's willingness to respond to your needs and wants. To that extent, successful romantic relationships are give-and-take affairs. Black males are often stereotyped as being poor providers of emotional support. They are frequently depicted in the media as being uncaring, unfeeling, unemotional studs. In any event, black men and women who are in fact stingy with their feelings are making a big mistake. They undoubtedly are less influential in their romantic relationships than they would be if they gave more. They should realize that by being more of an emotional resource to their partners, they stand to gain significantly.

What isn't a stereotype, however, is the fact that black men, more often than black women, are conditioned to believe that the only way to increase their power in romantic relationships is to increase the number of material assets they provide their partners. On this point, black men are mistaken—mainly because black women often have as much to give in the way of financial wherewithal as black men. And material rewards aren't always what these women want most in a relationship.

I listened to Dorothy, an assistant hospital administrator, size up the problem. Strikingly good looking, with long eyelashes and a square jaw, Dorothy said, "What I value most is someone to be close to. I meet far too many men who try to substitute material goods for their unwillingness or inability to address my social and emotional needs." A smile played around Dorothy's mouth as she said, "The men don't seem to realize that there are other ways to gain influence with me than through material rewards. Most women I know can buy their own material rewards! What men need to learn to do is pay more attention to my feelings. I don't need gold chains and watches. I look for *feeling*. I don't mind being surprised with a rose once in a while. I like to be remembered on my birthday. But more than that, I settle for being asked how my day went. I want a man who can lift my spirits when I have the blues."

Sex

Consider this: Don said that he knows his girlfriend Joan exerts too much influence in their relationship. His friend Mike asked him why he permits her to exercise so much power. Don was clearly embarrassed. He finally stated the reason: Joan is dynamite in bed.

The power of sex, some would argue, can be the greatest of all resources exchanged between romantic partners. It is without doubt one of our greatest motivators. The expression "whipped" is but a crude way of stating that one partner in a relationship is being controlled by the sexual power of the other. Indeed, given the risks individuals take with their lives, fortunes, and careers in order to have sex with their desired partners, sex is clearly an important and powerful factor in most people's lives.

Your level of influence in your relationships may be affected considerably by how sexually satisfying you are to your partners, and how satisfying they are to you. For some, the ability to satisfy the sexual desires of their partners is their main basis of power within romantic relationships. Like Don, however, most of us would hate to admit that our partner is able to control us with sex. But in reality this often happens. Those who are good lovers are apt to experience greater power in their relationships than those who are not. Typically, of course, everyone thinks that he or she is a great lover; however, as with everything else, some of us are and some of us ain't.

Money, Things, And Social Status

You may be thinking, "What? More talk about money? Is this guy obsessed with money?" I hope not. While I do recognize that couples have a host of other issues that affect their perceptions of a fair relationship, I also recognize that money, along with sex, is one of the most common problems noted by black couples. In spite of the lower emphasis that people like Dorothy place on tangible rewards, there is a lot to be said about the advantages of material assets in a relationship, as Walter can attest. Thirty years out of Morehouse, Walter is successful by anybody's standards, and has many assets that women desire. By day, he makes his appointed rounds to his chain of beauty supply stores in his specially painted silver Miata. By night, he drives his Mercedes-Benz coupe, and he usually is accompanied by an exceptionally attractive, statuesque "twentysomething" who seems to have as much fun with him as she would with any man half his age. Walter's "secret" is his wealth. His is an example of how your material assets can enhance your attractiveness to others. Obviously Walter and his youthful companion each have things that the other finds desirable, and which they use to exert considerable influence over each other.

Money easily translates into power, as Walter's case demonstrates. In general, those partners who have more money to spend have a greater ability to influence the behavior of their romantic partners. Having more money increases your romantic power because it allows you to cater to people who desire partners who are financially well off. Money, social status, and prestige all have similar effects on people who want to be upwardly mobile and share in the benefits of the so-called "rich and famous." Hence, by obtaining wealth or prestige, people typically become more attractive to others, and are able to utilize that attraction to get others to do things for them.

The economic resources that enable people to own sports cars, expensive stereos, spacious apartments or homes, and fine clothes are often important because possessions like these are likely to attract a variety of potential romantic partners. But let me add a proviso to those who think money is the answer to their romantic difficulties: sharing your resources with a potential partner does not guarantee that this person will fall in love with you! That person is likely to be attracted to you, though, and this attraction is likely to enhance your power over them. Is it always good to have more resources than those partners over whom you wish to exert influence? Not necessarily. But in general an abundance of the "right" resources relative to those of your partner will likely influence how much power you will be able to exert within your relationship. As I have mentioned, the relative economic equality among male and female black singles may be more problematic than it is beneficial in terms of relationships.

The case of Arthur and Tremaine illustrates this point. A muscular assistant high school football coach, Arthur is traditional in his views about black male-female relationships. "I'm like most black men in that I'm in a serious struggle to obtain personal and professional respect from the society at large," he said. "Everything I see around me tells me that as a man I am supposed to be the chief breadwinner and decision-maker in a relationship. I guess that's why I'm super sensitive to any notion that challenges that assumption. Tremaine and I earn a good living together, but I get a little upset at times by her take-charge attitude."

Tremaine, a systems analyst, looked at him with a demure smile as she said, "I don't mind letting Arthur make the major decisions, but I think I should at least be consulted. I have to remind him that I bring in as much money as a he does. I know society used to say that women shouldn't be as financially and professionally well off as their men, but that's no longer the way things are in many black relationships."

Arthur and Tremaine will have to find common ground on this issue if their relationship is to survive. Tremaine's attitude shows how the superior financial resources that black women often bring to a relationship can result in these women demanding equal—or even greater—power than their partners. This higher income, and concomitantly greater professional status, has resulted in black women like Tremaine sometimes being perceived as domineering and threatening. Which is why Arthur admits that, "I feel like I have less influence with her than I had with women who were less well off. It was only after I developed a close relationship with Tremaine that I began to feel I wasn't quite the man of the house, so to speak, or the decision-maker that I had always imagined myself being in any relationship."

Therein lies a major problem black couples must address. They need to understand the implications of their unique situation. Because black men like Arthur are often no longer the sole wage earners in their relationships, it is unfair of them to expect their partners to sit quietly and allow the men to make all the important decisions that affect both of them. Black men must understand, too, that romantic relationships, like most other relationships, follow the second Golden Rule: "He (or she) who has the gold makes the rule."

The equality in Arthur's relationship with Tremaine is perceived by Arthur as an inadequacy. Arthur isn't alone in his traditional views. There are many women out there who feel their male partners should pay most or all of the bills. Arthur's case is mirrored by that of Mark, a curly-haired, smoothed-skinned accountant who related to me what he perceived to be a humiliating story involving Michelle, his partner.

One Saturday evening, the couple had gone to a movie and then had dinner. Mark paid for everything, and when they returned to Michelle's house, he expected her to follow their normal procedure of reimbursing him for part of the expenses. When she never got around to doing it, he politely asked for the money. Let Mark tell the rest: "She immediately got a real attitude. I could tell this had been bothering her a long time. She put her hands on her hips, man, and reminded me that she deserved a great deal of credit because she was bringing in more money than any woman was supposed to. In so many words, she said men and women should not be financial equals. By that she meant that I somehow was not up to par and—get this—I should be glad to have her. Then she goes through this bag about how I should be less demanding in our relationship. Sisters can be a real trip, can't they?"

Listening to Mark reminded me of a conversation I'd heard between two other men, John and Leo, after each had argued with his partner over who should have the most say in a relationship. Leo exclaimed, "Man, our women should stop saying that we ask too much from them. These women just don't know—they should be glad to have us. Just having a job is a miracle, given the economic conditions and levels of discrimination we face. Even if we bring in a little less than they do, it's still more than many brothers have. And given that there are so many sisters out there without men, they should be happy to go along with our programs." "Yeah," agreed Leo, who was quick to point out, "There are a lot more women like them than men like us."

The above discussions are common characterizations of male-female disputes over power as depicted by black men. The solution is simple, but it is often difficult for many black men to swallow. In situations where black men and women have comparable incomes, black women should expect to have a substantial degree of influence in their relationships. Things are no longer the way your parents may have told you they were supposed to be. Black men must realize that, if their partners want greater input into the decisions regarding their romantic relationship, they do not become less of a man by agreeing to share the power.

By the same token, black women must recognize that the situation for many black men runs counter to what women were conditioned to assume. It is not so much that most men mind sharing power equally, but rather that men sometimes have difficulty with what they believe this equality says about them. That is, they have been taught that such equality means they are somehow less than the men they should be, not totally in charge of their romantic relationships, if they can't make all the major decisions. In addition, black women should resist thinking that a romantic partner is inferior because he earns less money than they. Things are tough for significant numbers of black men. They often face very different economic realities than other men. Therefore, black women must attempt to evaluate who is a good or poor romantic partner on the basis of the realities of black life, rather than on the basis of what they traditionally have been encouraged to think.

Despite the changes in what is acceptable for black men and women of the nineties, it is still considered less socially acceptable for a woman to have more to offer her partner in the way of economic resources than he has to offer her. Such situations are common among black dating couples, however. They present a unique challenge to black couples, again because they run counter to the cultural expectation that men should have more education, money, and status than their female partners.

Black women frequently state that many black men shy away from dating women who have the potential to exercise substantial influence in their romantic relationships. This is true to some extent. Most black men would have difficulty dating a woman who has the economic resources of someone like Oprah Winfrey. To many men, it might initially seem like a great romantic opportunity, but it would soon dawn on them that in comparison to most of their prior romantic relationships, they'd have less influence in this one. While it is possible for a romantic relationship in which the female has more financial resources (and power) than the male to survive, it requires a very strong sense of personal worth on the part of the male, and considerable sensitivity on the part of the female. The black woman in such instances must constantly stay in tune with the ways her greater resources and greater power are affecting her partner. Among other things, this may call for the couple to find ways to minimize the influence of money in their dating activities. For example, an average-wage-earning male might feel uncomfortable if the couple frequently went to restaurants where the tab for two was, for instance, over $100. Hence, when possible, money should not be the determining factor as to where couples eat, go, or play.

Personality And Beauty

You already know that the personal characteristics of your romantic partners may allow them to exert considerable influence in your life. You may find such qualities as honesty, wit, sincerity, humor, or intelligence irresistibly attractive. You often refer to those who are capable of influencing you with their charisma, personal magnetism, and forceful arguments as having "strong" personalities. Personal attributes such as these are powerful assets that people who possess them frequently use to get their way.

Although we discussed the importance of beauty earlier, its mention is warranted here also. Beauty is a power resource for those who possess it. Remember Walter, the Mercedes-driving businessman, and his attractive young girlfriend? It is reasonable to assume that at least some of Walter's attraction to his young date is because of her physical beauty. What power she has in their relationship is largely derived from her physical attractiveness. You are probably thinking that she may be exerting sexual influence as well, and you are probably right. But for someone who wants to be noticed, as is obviously the case with Walter (considering his choice of cars), his date's striking level of physical attractiveness may be as important—if not more important—to him as sex. Beauty can be used like other personal assets—to win friends and influence people. The more of it you have and the more your romantic partners value it, the more influential you are likely to be with them.

Assistance And Companionship (Spending Time)

Thus far we have noted some of the personal and physical assets that people commonly use as resources in their attempts to influence each other. However, in many cases just being available to spend time with your romantic partners is likely to make you important and influential with them. Those people who spend the most time talking and doing things with you are very likely to become your friends. Indeed research suggests that sharing activities with people is perhaps the most important factor in enhancing their attraction to you. Persons who are willing to accompany you to those activities or events that interest you—for example, to watch Michael Jordan perform magic on the court or listen to author Terry McMillan discuss her work—may become especially dear to you. In short, people who are willing to share their time with you (not just their goodies) have a good chance of becoming influential in your life.

This point is best illustrated through the relationship of Mary and Ralph. Though she is plain looking, does little to enhance her physical appearance, is far from stylish in her dress, and doesn't earn much money working as a short-order cook at a soul-food restaurant, Mary is a jewel in Ralph's eyes. His friends occasionally ask why it is that Mary is able to get him to do things other women could not. Indeed, she has considerable influence with Ralph, despite the fact that she does not in any way enhance Ralph's prestige or social status. "Mary," he told his friends, "is always willing to help me with the little things in my life. Some people are all too willing to spend my money, but they are never around when I need them. Once I had to go into the hospital after I came down with what I thought was pneumonia. It turned out to be just a bad cold. The doctor put me in the hospital so suddenly that I didn't have time to take care of minor things, like mailing some bills and calling my employer. I called quite a few 'friends,' and you'd be surprised how many of them found excuses not to do simple favors for me, or even drop by to visit. But not Mary. She handled these things like a pro. I decided then and there that this was the kind of woman I was looking for, a woman who didn't mind taking a little time, didn't mind sharing. That really won me over."

As the saying goes, we all need someone to do something for us sometime. That something might be a personal favor, an offer of good advice, or some other kind of assistance. Those who help you with such difficult tasks as moving, painting, fixing your car, or finding a new apartment are likely to enhance their levels of influence with you. Because they help you, you are likely to reciprocate by helping them. There is little doubt that those romantic partners who give you their time or help are more influential with you than those who don't.

Use Your Power With Style

Thus far we have looked primarily at those things that enhance your power in romantic relationships, but the manner in which you exercise that power is also important. We have all met people who were able to get us to do things without our feeling resentful or angry for obliging them. Although they frequently did have resources with which to entice us, they also tended to have nice ways of approaching us for a favor. In short, they exercised their power with style.

In general, styles of exerting power can be characterized according to three types:

• "soft" strategies, such as manipulation, flattery, seduction, and appearing helpless;

• "hard" strategies, such as insisting, threatening, bullying, and claiming greater knowledge;

• "neutral" strategies, such as "bargaining," which is most likely to be employed when couples have similar access to resources (namely income), and "disengagement" by sulking or leaving the scene of a situation in which there is disagreement (something, by the way, men are more apt to do than women).

Not surprisingly the persistent use of hard tactics, such as bullying or threatening, is likely to damage and disrupt your romantic relationships more so than the use of soft or neutral tactics, such as flattery or bargaining with your romantic partners. Power struggles are common to all interpersonal relationships. However, power struggles with your romantic partners are often counterproductive to your overall romantic goals. Even when we think that we have "won," ours is a pyrrhic victory. You may have gotten your way (some need or desire met), but the damage to your relationship was more costly than what you obtained from your victory.

Take, for example, the following situation involving Oliver and Pearl. They had plans to go to a movie. She wanted to see a love story and he a war movie. Oliver came down hard for his position, stating that given that he always paid, Pearl should go along with his wishes. This annoyed and embarrassed her. They went to see the war movie, but she took revenge by giving him the silent treatment afterward. That led to a big fight. Oliver got his way by employing a form of bullying. In doing so, he alienated Pearl.

Try A Little Tenderness

Winning may be the only thing that counts in football, but that isn't the case in romance. Many of us employ in our romantic lives the harder strategies that we have previously found to be beneficial in our professional lives. This is a serious mistake. We may have found that the use of hard strategies often gets us what we want in the workplace. The key difference between these two situations is that in your professional relationships you generally do not care if your adversary likes or loves you at the end of the struggle. On the contrary, in romantic relationships you want your partners to at least like you when you conclude some negotiation with them.

The use of hard power strategies with their partners may account for some singles becoming increasingly more successful in their professional lives while becoming increasingly less so with their romantic partners. Many may be practicing styles of relating to their partners that may be good for business, but bad for romance.

Romantic relationships are formed and maintained, at least in part, according to your ability to get along with your partners. Your power struggles are minimized if you are highly compatible with your partner, if the two of you want to do and experience the same things. The consequences of your romantic power struggles are also minimized if you are able to employ nonoffensive ways of exercising power.

Review the above definitions of different power strategies and ask yourself which ones you are most likely to use in your own romantic life. Think of the last five situations in which you attempted to influence your partner; then ask yourself the following three questions about each of those situations (and ask your partner if he or she agrees with your answers).

1. What was your need or want from your partner?
2. What hard, soft, or neutral strategy did you use to get your partner to satisfy your need or want?
3. What was the outcome of your effort?

The outcomes you've observed in these situations should give you some idea of which strategies work and which fail. If you find that you are consistently employing hard strategies, decide if it's worth winning the individual battles, but then frequently losing the romantic war.

The odds are good that as a black person you take quite a beating in your attempts to get ahead in life. The fact is, however, that your potential partners do, too. James Baldwin once suggested that for a black person to have even a modest amount of racial awareness is to be in a constant rage. Black couples must be careful not to manifest this rage in their interactions with each other. You must remember that the brother or sister you are dating is not "the system." Be gentle in your attempts to influence your partner.

Those men and women who want successful relationships must rely on bargaining as their key power strategy. Thus, as a means to improve their relationships, they must abandon hard, domineering power styles. For example, if you shout, stop it; if you are inclined to claim greater knowledge of a situation (typically something men do), break the habit; if you bully and threaten, cut the bull; if you are overly insistent, or tempted to insist on insisting, don't. Learn instead to bargain, reason, flatter, and seduce. Above all, strive for fairness.

Winning every dispute—even if you can—is unlikely to endear you to your romantic partners. Ideally, you and your partner will find each other irreplaceable because of the unique constellation of personal qualities each of you brings to the relationship. This is likely to give each of you comparable degrees of influence within the relationship, because neither of you would want to lose the other. The perception between partners that the other is difficult to replace tends to equalize power within relationships, and also tends to stabilize relationships by increasing the partners' commitment to each other.

Grudges

It seems advisable, at least in romantic relationships, to have a short memory. Don't hold on to the details and feelings left over from previous disputes. Doing so can be counterproductive to new beginnings. If you bring the baggage of every old romantic dispute to each new disagreement, you will soon find yourself overreacting to everything.

I am not suggesting that you become a doormat, but I am suggesting that—as with a doormat—you sweep yourself off once in a while. Hence, not only do I advocate that you employ softer or more neutral strategies in your efforts to get your needs met, but that you try not to hold grudges.

I asked a friend of mine who had gone through a particularly bad romantic break what she had learned from the experience. She told me that people must decide in a relationship which is more important: holding on to the feelings of anger that occur during the course of romantic power struggles, or holding on to the romance. I felt this was a fine way of putting it. The ability to let go of anger is a real romantic asset. To be more successful in romantic relationships, we must quickly learn to give our partners the benefit of the doubt. After all, neither of you is likely to be the one doing the right thing every single time.

10 A Positive Outlook

MOST PEOPLE who have good luck in the romantic marketplace have one main thing going for them: they like people, and it shows. Having a positive attitude is fundamental to attracting potential partners. Moreover, increasing the numbers of potential dates you meet is unlikely to help you much if, once in their company, they find that you have a funky attitude. Hence, in addition to being in the right place, at the right time, you must be there with the right attitude. Research has consistently shown that everyone "likes a liker." In fact, if others perceive that you like them, they are more likely to like you. They are also likely to disclose more about themselves, disagree with you less, express greater similarity to you, and do all these things in a more pleasant manner.

Obviously this sort of behavior is important to establishing romantic relationships. Yet it is often the case that we expect others to demonstrate a positive attitude toward us before we will demonstrate a positive attitude toward them. It's important to realize that demonstrating a positive attitude seems to create a positive loop, which goes something like this: We feel good about others and, therefore, behave positively toward them. This increases the probability that they will feel and behave positively toward us, which in turn makes us feel good about ourselves.

There is a lot to be gained from believing that you are a likable person, and behaving in a likable way. You should, therefore, have positive feelings about yourself before venturing into the romantic marketplace. Sigmund Freud believed that in order to love others, it was first necessary to learn to love yourself. Persons who don't feel good about themselves are likely to have difficulty feeling good about others, and in turn getting others to feel good about them. If you feel good about yourself, you will feel more confident and less threatened by others, and be more likely to acknowledge their positive features. As a result you will behave more kindly toward them. In contrast, if you feel negatively about yourself, you are inclined to be less giving and supportive of others, for fear that such generosity would somehow diminish your stature. Anyone who has dated people who did not feel good about themselves has probably witnessed how difficult it is for them to compliment other people. They just don't seem to have anything positive to spare.

Unquestionably, not feeling good about yourself seriously reduces the likelihood that others will like you. However, an absence of self-liking is often not the problem for dating singles of 1990s. Instead, a greater problem is that many singles like themselves too much and others not enough. While Freud asserted that we need to love ourselves *first*, it seems that some of us must have thought he said we should love ourselves *only*. This is a problem for many professional black singles. Many of them may have been the first of their race to make accomplishments in certain fields. Their successes can cause them to think too well of themselves and not well enough of others.

The Negative Loop

Some singles, it seems, have gotten stuck in a negative loop with respect to their attitudes on liking and being liked by people they meet. For example, we have all been in the company of people who find something bad to say about almost everyone who walks within their line of vision. In fact, you may have found yourself afraid to leave their company, for fear that when you did they would have something less than flattering to say about you. What you may not have noticed about these individuals, however, is that often they don't have many friends or romantic partners. Typically you'll find people like these gathered together in small groups, sharing their negative perceptions about other people. *Stay away from these people!* They are, so to speak, "scaring the fish away." Instead of hanging out with these downbeats, find a friend or two who think better of other people. Not only will you find that being around those with positive attitudes will help you attract more romantic attention, but you'll also have a better time doing it.

The Luck Factor

When I was a boy, my dad used to say to me that "it was better to be born lucky than rich." I never really thought too much about this old-time cliche until I became aware of what psychologists have identified as the "luck factor." People whom other people like tend to have consistently good luck, because they are beneficiaries of the luck factor. They are apt to have an extensive network of people who like them. These friends and acquaintances turn them on to all sorts of things: tips on good jobs, where to find the best deals, et cetera. It stands to reason that these friends and acquaintances also turn them on to the best people, so to speak.

For many, the luck factor comes naturally, but it can be developed. You can learn to harness the world's greatest resource—people. In short, having an extensive network of friends can help you fulfill your romantic needs. The luck factor can be crucial, as your meeting of new potential partners will often come about through the efforts of those who know and like you rather than just through chance meetings on your own. Subsequently, anyone who likes you—ranging from your colleagues at work to your mail carrier—is of potential assistance in your effort to find romantic partners.

Thus it is a good idea to be positive in your attitude toward people. Remember, no one wants to be held responsible for introducing a friend to someone who has a bad attitude. It pays to be positive even when you're interacting with someone you would never associate with your search for a romantic partner. For example, an elderly man or woman who rides the bus with you each morning, or your barber or beautician, may have a son, daughter, nephew, or niece who is just tailor-made for you.

Don't Take An Old Attitude On A New Date

"The problem with all you black men/women is . . . " How often have you heard black men and women begin, and often end, conversations in this fashion? I have rarely found those who employ such gender stereotypes to be successful in their romantic lives. Who wants to start off a relationship apologizing for being a man or a woman? As a black single hoping to find romance, you must resist the temptation to make negative generalizations about black men and women. When expecting the worse, you will invariably prove yourself right. We have all known friends and lovers who continue to create the same negative romantic situations for themselves. They bring their old negative attitudes to each of their new relationships. They are, so to speak, fighting old wars with new partners—and not surprisingly, they generally lose! Few of us are willing to pay for the romantic sins or misfortunes of others. Each of us has been hurt in our own prior romantic experiences. Yet, despite our past romantic disappointments, most of us are able to make peace both with ourselves and those with whom we were involved. At least, we are able to put our prior relationships into perspective—far enough behind us to avoid acting out our old romantic disputes with each new partner.

While none of us is completely unaffected by our prior romantic histories, some of us are better at starting over than others. If you are to be successful at establishing new romantic relationships, you must be willing to enter them with an upbeat attitude, even if your romantic past has been difficult. You must attempt to see your new partners in a positive light. You must actively search out those qualities you would most like to find in a person. By displaying a positive attitude regarding your expectations of a partner, you will increase the probability that you will find one. In effect, this will help create positive, self-fulfilling romantic prophecies.

Don't expect your new romantic partner to supply you with this positive attitude. You must bring a positive attitude of your own to your new romantic relationship. Speaking of one of her personal romantic relationships, Susan Taylor, editor of *Essence* magazine, made this point when she stated in one of her columns, "I learned that a relationship can't make you happy, you must bring your happiness with you." This is emphatically true.

Let Your Attitude Show

So often we fail to demonstrate adequately how we feel. Merely thinking positively is not enough—our romantic partners can't read our minds. We must let our positive attitude show. The following are but a few of the many ways that you can demonstrate your positive attitude toward those you date.

• Have a positive presence of self. You should look, smell, and dress well—it should be apparent to everyone that you have a good self-image. You should speak favorably of others (especially in their absence). As we noted above, people like people whom they believe like other people.

• Give sincere compliments to your dates. Attempt to take notice of qualities that are unique to them. Pay attention to small details (everyone has already noticed that he or she is handsome/beautiful). For example, maybe his new glasses really complement his mustache, or the color of her ring highlights her shapely hands. Most importantly, your compliments should be factual, and if possible something that few have probably taken time to notice. There's no need to use "lines," or say things that aren't true.

• Have a good sense of humor (loosen-up, don't be a tight-ass!). How many times have you heard people say of their partners that they liked them because they made them laugh? Having a good sense of humor is surely one of the best things that can be thought of you by those you want to like you. It is believed that laughter is not only enjoyable in itself, but good for our mental health as well. So, when possible, tell a funny story and make your date laugh. You may be thinking, "But I don't tell stories or jokes well." It doesn't matter—even if you screw up the telling of a story, your date will probably still laugh at how you told it. This will also allow him or her to see that you don't take yourself too seriously. At a minimum, let your date know that you like to laugh, given the opportunity. Failing to be humorous yourself, take your date to see a funny movie. Finally, learn to laugh at yourself and not just at your partner! This is critical. For example, have you noticed that popular people are frequently telling others of how something crazy or ridiculous has once again just happened to them?

• Be thoughtful. Do the little things that everyone wishes someone else would do for them. A good place to start is to remember a birthday, favorite color, or special occasion. Comment on places and things the two of you did on your prior dates. For example, can you remember what he or she wore, or something nice that he or she said? Following your first date, you may consider sending a card, or flowers, or just calling to thank your partner for a great time.

• Be optimistic. Attempt to see the up side of things in your discussions of people and events. Try to see the glass of water as being half full rather than half empty. Few of us like a sour puss. People who always see the negative side of the intentions of people or life's events bring us down. In a word, be like your attitude—positive.

11 Between Dates: Down-Time Ain't Necessarily Bad Time

Y OUR DATING LIFE is prone to follow a feast-or-famine schedule. There are times when you probably have more individuals interested in making your acquaintance than you can handle. And then there are other times when it seems as though romance has forsaken you once and for all—you can't buy a date. It's as though you've run into a romantic drought—no one seems to be of interest, nor interested in you. When you first experienced such a down-turn in your love life, you were probably terrified, believing that you had seen the last of romance. Then, weeks or perhaps even months later, you probably found yourself right back in love again. With the passage of time you have perhaps come to recognize that these periods of feast and famine are cyclical in nature. Most certainly, an awareness that romance will, in all probability, come again makes it possible (almost) to avoid panicking during these romantic dry spells.

Once you end a relationship with someone with whom you have been accustomed to spending large blocks of your day, you are likely to find yourself having considerable amounts of free time on your hands. You may not be quite sure exactly what to do with it all. Sometimes you may try to catch up on your sleep, or attempt to clean up your home. While activities such as these are good for about a week, they are unlikely to carry you through a romantic down period of several months or so. Of course, you could elect to pine away waiting for that next romance, or you could rush out into the dating scene and attempt to force the issue by dating someone you don't really like. Instead of employing either of these strategies, you could put your romantic down-time to good use.

I have thus far given considerable attention to the idea of Romantic Market Value (RMV), which again is the sum of all the personal assets you bring to your interpersonal relationships. Your RMV is like all other assets in that its value is subject to change. A change in your RMV can occur because what you have to offer has become more or less common. For example, moving to a new city with fewer numbers of desirable romantic partners can change the degree to which you are sought out as a partner.

Changes in your RMV can also occur because *you* have changed. You, in effect, can influence the romantic market conditions you face by making yourself more desirable. Most of us have spent considerable amounts of time attempting to improve ourselves with the hope of getting more out of life. It seems obvious that the more we have to offer, in the way of education, intelligence, charm, and income, the more we can expect to obtain in return. This same principle applies to our ability to attract romantic partners. In other words, given that singles are likely to seek out the most desirable dates, then the more desirable you become as a potential partner, the more desirable a romantic partner you should be able to attract.

There are highs and lows, ups and downs in most of our romantic lives. Little need be said about the up-times, as they are often the best times in our lives. However, the down-times need not be bad times either. You can turn these romantic droughts into periods of personal growth and development. Indeed, periods between romantic partners provide an excellent opportunity for you to enhance your overall level of romantic desirability. You should always attempt to come out of each down-period with more personal strengths and assets than you had when you went into them. You should learn to use your down-times to enhance yourself in ways that will make you even more sought after in the romantic marketplace.

What Should You Work On?

Each of us has personal strengths and weaknesses that affect our romantic relationships. Which aspects of yourself you elect to work on will, of course, depend on where you feel you need the most improvement, and what, at the time, you would most enjoy doing. There are any number of areas where most of us can use some improvement, some of which I discuss below. However, the following considerations are not intended to be an exhaustive list, as you must determine for yourself the areas in which you can make improvements.

Social Skills

This is perhaps the broadest area on which you can focus. Such things as charm, wit, humor, and verbal and listening skills come under this heading. We could all stand to improve our basic interaction skills with people—learning to listen better, increasing our ability to communicate our feelings and thoughts, being more courteous and polite. You could attempt to improve these and other social skills by attending weekend workshops or joining groups designed for that purpose. There are also self-help books available to aid you in becoming more socially skillful.

Because it is best to interact with others while attempting to improve social skills, reading materials should be supplemented with some real-life practice. I strongly suggest that, if possible, you join a group whose purpose it is to improve social skills. The key, however, is not just to interact with others, but to receive feedback on your interaction skills and how to improve them. This, I believe, is best done in some sort of group setting with others who are working on similar issues.

Education

There is no substitute for a good education. Being well educated greatly contributes to your overall desirability as a romantic partner. In fact, improving your level of education is likely to strengthen a number of areas that are important in your attempts to attract more interesting and exciting romantic partners. Obtaining more education is likely to bolster your status in the job market, as well as your desirability in the romantic market.

So, you might ask, who wants to sleep with an Einstein or W.E.B. DuBois? Lots of people! Many people are turned on by the depth of their mate's intellect and know-how. Romantic down-time is often a good time to take courses in art history, philosophy, music appreciation, or any number of other subjects. Education, in general, tends to enhance our understanding of the world and simultaneously increase the interest others find in us. Furthermore, romantic down-time may be a good opportunity to return to school to start (or finish) that advanced degree!

Income

Increasing our income is, for most of us, always a good step. Specifically, making more money is likely to make us more attractive to others. We have all seen people who clearly would not have drawn such desirable partners were it not for their economic success. Given greater resources we can afford to experience things we may not be able to otherwise, such as trips, evenings at the theater, and dinners out. In addition, our ability to command greater financial resources often enhances our self-esteem and the perceptions others have of us. Thus, a period between dates may be a good opportunity to look for a better job or pursue investment opportunities.

Physical Appeal

Down-time may be the right time to get in good shape. It might be a good idea to enroll in an aerobics class or physical fitness program. It may also be a good time to have our teeth straightened, try a new hair style, or grow a beard (Why not? After all, you don't have a partner to criticize you if she doesn't like it). It may also be a good time to rethink your wardrobe—is it too conservative? Too juvenile? Improving your physical appearance will influence how others respond to you. However, a word of caution—don't believe that being good looking is the first and final word in romance. Spend some time working on this aspect of yourself, if you think you need it, but you eventually will reach a point of diminishing returns. In fact, for many of us, time spent attempting to increase our physical attractiveness would be better spent in other ways.

Be honest with yourself. You know the areas in which you need improvement. I don't mean getting a new hairstyle or buying a new suit. I mean more fundamental things, such as toning your body through exercise. It is estimated that 70 percent of black women and 50 percent of black men are overweight. Shedding those pounds would make a significant number of us more physically appealing. Just by not being obese, you have an asset that many of your potential competitors don't when seeking out desirable partners. Losing weight, then, might be your best strategy for enhancing your RMV.

Mystique

We have all met people who have attended good schools, gone into solid professions, and have the right friends—and yet they bore our socks off. They have what we might call a low mystique quotient. They may know a great deal, but they rarely know anything very interesting. There is nothing about them that makes us want to get to know them better. Moreover, they might have looked great wearing "designer everything," and, yet, they came off more or less like everyone else. In short, they had no intrigue or mystique about them. In this sense, having more of what everyone else has is not necessarily better.

In contrast, if you think of the people in your life who have fascinated you most, they often knew or could do things which were unusual. Somehow it helps to be different in interesting ways. Thus, periods between dates may be a good time to enhance your mystique quotient. Such things as performing magic tricks, reading palms or tea leaves, speaking a foreign language well, knowing the history of unique words, expressions, or superstitions, or being able to quote fables and parables about life make us more interesting as people. Even being able to perform a good card trick or to tell unusually funny or exciting stories will help others to see you as being unique, more interesting and, hence, more desirable to be around. Perhaps one of the best things about improving yourself in these ways is that they tend to be permanent and lasting.

Mental Health

Studies show that individuals who have good mental health are likely to pair off with each other, as are individuals with poor mental health. In the interest of attracting romantic partners who are themselves mentally healthy, we may want to ensure that our own emotional condition is good. Unquestionably, seeking a professional counselor with whom to discuss our problems and concerns is, invariably, a sign of good mental health and maturity. Most of us have psychological concerns that we would like to overcome. For example, we may be somewhat closed off emotionally; have difficulty expressing our feelings to others; or suffer from shyness. There may be long-standing familial, sexual, or other issues in your life that you would like to resolve. A break from intense romantic involvement may be a good time to pursue these areas of growth.

Worldliness

No one wants to be a local yokel—most certainly, no one wants to date one. Growth in terms of greater worldliness is enhanced most by travel or by reading about places to travel. The places to which you travel need not be in Africa or Europe. Even a trip to another city is likely to point out to you how people and things are often done differently elsewhere. In fact, seeing towns and cities other than your own will give you a broader perspective on life. You will gain insight into how other people live, work, and carry out their lives. Having some sense of worldliness will help you avoid being narrow-minded and provincial. Travel is also likely to make you more interesting, in that you are apt to see things on your journeys that many others have not, and which may be interesting to them. Down-time between romantic partners may be an excellent time to get away from it all. Go visit that aunt in Chicago, or that old high school buddy in Los Angeles, or, if you have some extra money, take a cruise. Even getting away for a few days can be refreshing and enlightening.

Spirituality

Being less intensely involved with others for a while is often a good opportunity to get in touch with your spiritual self. This may consist of establishing formal religious ties, or may merely involve your getting in touch with your thoughts and feelings about life and existence. Development in this area is likely to make you more at peace with yourself and make others more at peace with you. You might put your romantic down-time to good use in renewing your religious faith, or rediscovering what meaning life has for you.

Social And Political Awareness

Getting involved in social and civic activities can be a rewarding break from the singles scene. Being concerned with the welfare of others is

147

also likely to give you a break from being too concerned with yourself, something most of us are inclined to do if we spend too much time alone. A political activist I know of once overheard some people discussing how bored they were with life and his comment to them was that he would be bored also, if he thought only about himself all the time.

Becoming a role model for black kids, teaching the illiterate to read, finding shelter for homeless families, or working on any number of exciting campaigns for up-and-coming black politicians will serve you well. Activities such as these will provide you with a break from your own concerns, and at the same time introduce you to new issues, places, and people. As a result of helping others, you are likely to feel better about yourself and add a new and enlightened dimension to your character. You may even want to run for some civic or political office yourself. Such an experience can have a wealth of potential social and personal benefits.

Network

Sometimes romantic involvement can cause us to neglect our social support system. During a romance, you may find yourself visiting your family and best friends less regularly than usual. However, romantic down-time provides you with the opportunity to re-establish old sources of personal support. Romantic down-time is also a good time to write those long overdue letters. In addition to being useful in their own right, these activities have a strong potential for secondary payoff. Keep in mind that you probably met most of your previous dates through the introductions of others. By strengthening your social support network you are likely to increase your probabilities of meeting new potential partners.

You can always find reasons why you don't have time to engage in any of the above suggestions. However, most of these will serve to make you feel better about yourself, and enhance your desirability as a romantic partner. Furthermore, pursuing any of these suggestions beats going into a state of social withdrawal and depression simply because there is no new love on your romantic horizon.

Also, this discussion has focused largely on efforts to improve yourself and to broaden your outlook in order to become more desirable to other singles. However, engaging in these suggested activities will also help to make you a better person, the kind who is sought after—and difficult to find—in the romantic marketplace.

12 Liking, Loving, And Lusting

DO YOU LIKE, LOVE, OR LUST after your romantic partner? If you experience all three of these emotions, consider yourself lucky. Each can complement the others, and all can have a positive effect on your romantic relationship. Lust, for example, can trigger excitement, desire, and affection. Lust is like a spark that can get the engine of romance moving. How far it takes you depends on whether your initial raw feelings contain the elements of something more permanent.

Meanwhile, the emotion of "like" helps you sustain romance when a relationship begins to sputter and stall during the inevitable interpersonal conflicts that can make the romantic journey difficult. As we shall discuss, there are important differences between loving and liking a person. We also shall see that some people love their partners even though they do not like them. In any case, all of these emotions can be equally important to romance. That's why it's essential to appreciate all three of them, and to understand better the roles they play in your romantic relationship.

Lust: Jump Starter For Romance

The thing to remember about lust is that it has nothing to do with anything else except what you see and how you feel at that moment. Lust is first and foremost sexual attraction. It is what many men feel after they turn to the swimsuit centerfold in *Jet* magazine. It is the swept-away emotion that seizes some women when they watch Denzel Washington in a movie scene. Lust, in short, is the uninhibited desire to ravish someone in the complete absence of any other information about the person, except for the fact that he or she turns you on. Are you merely lusting after your romantic partner? You are, if most everything you want to do with him or her involves sex, or if your description of your partner to friends consists primarily of his or her sex-related assets, skills, talents, or appetites.

All these attributes fit a long-winded old buddy of mine named Ernest, especially as he is when between romantic relationships. Our friendship goes back to the days when brothers wore bell bottoms and bushy haircuts and when Afro-coiffed sisters were into mini-skirts and go-go boots. Whenever Ernest mentioned having met yet another potential mini-skirted partner during those days, he would never fail to tell me about her breasts and the contour of her hips and legs before he got around to mentioning much else about her. It seemed that Ernest was born with lust in his heart. He told me once that it took an incident involving his cousin Claudia from Alabama to make him see how he was being ruled by his own lust.

Claudia lived in Luverne, a small town in Alabama. She would meet Ernest in Chicago at least one once a year for lunch at a certain soul-food joint that prepared collards and fried chicken just the way they did in Luverne. On one such occasion Claudia was late. Ernest had ordered and was eating, when he looked up as a sister was coming through the door. As he put it "Man, I dropped my drum stick like a dog who'd been chewing on an old bone and suddenly saw a piece of fresh meat." No, Ernest had not lusted after his own cousin. The woman who caught his eye was Alma, Claudia's friend, whom she had brought up with her from Alabama. According to Ernest, Alma was wearing a tight, black leather jump suit, zipped up the front just below her bosom. She had a body built like a crystal hour glass, and all Ernest could think about was having sex with her right there on the table, even though he didn't even know her name.

The behavior of brothers like Ernest is one reason why lust commonly receives a lot of bad press. But most of our romantic histories suggest that lust is a normal aspect of romance. For example, most of you are unlikely to accept the advances of would-be partners who do not turn you on. This does not mean that you want only sex; it just means that you are unlikely to date someone for whom you feel no "lust in your heart," even if you're too modest to admit it. Naturally, there are exceptions. We've all heard stories about people not being initially attracted to their partners. Moreover, people meet at work or are introduced under other circumstances that allow them to become acquainted without their first becoming romantically aroused. But the reverse is by far more common. Like Ernest, you cannot tell from across a room whether the target of your attraction is tender and caring. But you can tell if that person turns you on enough to want to know whether they are tender and caring.

Given Ernest's behavior, it's not surprising that most people are inclined to think of lust as a male emotion. Some say that black women do not lust after men, but my buddy Ernest says otherwise. "Any brother who has ever watched a sister at a Luther Vandross concert knows what I mean," he says. Ernest has also observed his cousin Claudia's lustful reaction to pictures of brothers in his body-building magazines. Her behavior surprised him, since she's very religious and because her manner gives the impression that she is somewhat shy. Even more surprising to him was how Claudia talked about how she would like get one of those guys in a Jacuzzi and do a lot more with him than enjoy the water.

Now you tell me: if "shy" cousin Claudia lusted after men that way, what do you think other women do? Many women would admit that Claudia's feelings are no different from their own. Such sentiments were expressed when I asked two women, Bertha and Leona, whether they thought women lusted after men in the same way that men lust after women. Although their responses may not be representative, their perceptions are not unique.

Bertha, a slightly built, middle-aged school teacher with a salt-and-pepper-colored natural hair style, has been divorced for some time, and the youngest of her three children is now in high school. She stays in great shape and maintains an active social life. There is little doubt, once you meet Bertha, that she is very much her own woman. She shows little concern for what others think. "I don't know who lusts more, but I do know that most women lust after men," she said. "You men think that you are the only ones interested in sex. But let me tell you it ain't so! If a man doesn't turn me on, or as my sister used to say, if I can't imagine him breathing heavy, then there is no sense of us getting anything started."

Leona is a tall, stylish sister in her early thirties. An assistant department store buyer, she's an up-and-coming buppie whose comments were of interest to me because she's from a rather reserved family, with parents who are university professors. She attended all the "right" schools and is part of a growing group of young black women who feel the sharp bite of the shortage of professional black men. When I heard her responses, I thought of Ernest's story about his cousin Claudia's spontaneous reaction to the male physique. "When I see certain guys in magazines, I tell myself I wish I could get with one of them," she said in a manner that belied her conservative upbringing. "But the man doesn't have to be built like Bo Jackson to turn me on. It may be a certain look. It can even be a suggestion of emotional sensitivity. So we women lust, yes! But I don't feel that we act on our lust as much as men do, since we might be socially inhibited from doing so, or we don't have as many opportunities to act."

Leona seems to have a great deal of support for her idea that women *express* lust less often than men, regardless of how they experience it. For one thing, men seem to experience lust with considerably less provocation. The woman need not be a physical knock-out of the Diahanne Carroll variety. She often need only look good in what she's wearing at the time, such as a tight skirt or sweater. In short, she need only have some particular aspect of her self that men find sexy. Moreover, men clearly respond more to visual stimulation than do women. This is perhaps most evident by the conventional male response to nude photographs of women. For men, sex itself is dependent on the arousal of lust. Rarely do men find compassion sexually arousing—important, yes, but sexually arousing, no! In contrast, women frequently report being sexually aroused solely by the emotional sensitivity and caring of their romantic partners.

Both black men and women are likely to tell you that they try to become friends before acting upon their feelings of lust. Make no mistake, though—lust is likely to be present first, awaiting the call to action. This is made most evident by the fact that so many couples have sex so early in their relationships. What seems to be occurring is that couples are often merely waiting for a respectable period of time to pass before acting on their mutual lust for each other.

Keep in mind my proviso that while lust can be helpful in jump-starting a relationship, it's usually only the first step toward something more permanent. Even the steamiest romantic relationship is unlikely to be sustained by lust alone. Moreover, there is no guarantee that lust will develop into anything else more substantive. Let me make it perfectly clear that I am not advocating that you always act on your feelings of lust. Such a recommendation would have all sorts of potentially negative social—and medical—implications, in addition to leaving you physically worn out all the time.

Lusting after your partners does not mean that you do not, or will never, love or like them. Based on my general conversations with black women, and the behavior of notorious lusters such as Ernest, I think black men need to be reminded that it is not their lust per se that bothers women, but rather the perception that black men feel nothing *more* than lust for their partners. And yet, few women would be offended if they learned that an appealing man lusted after them.

While lust is likely to be a big part of our romantic fantasies, most singles probably would argue that lust is of less importance than their liking or loving a partner. Yet lust tends to be sorely missed once it departs. And restoring it is not always easy. Indeed, finding ways to put sexual excitement back into our romantic lives has been a concern most of us have struggled with at one time or another. Therefore, don't think of lust as a phase you need to move beyond. Appreciate lust for what it is—a catalyst to and enhancer of romance.

But Are You In Love?

"I always know when I am 'in lust,' but am I in love?" a friend might ask. How do you know if you like or love a person? Even before the social psychologist Dr. Zick Rubin developed scales to measure the difference between liking and loving, Motown singers were crooning about what appears to be, at times, a seemingly contradictory phenomenon (Remember the song "You Really Got A Hold On Me," with the lyrics, "I don't like you, but I love you"?). Placing these two feelings in a different emotional context might help explain how this is possible. Think about parents and children. Parents may love all of their children, but they like some more than others. The same tendency occurs in romantic relationships. Partners love one another, though they might like one another less or not at all.

Love focuses foremost on our emotional feelings about our partner. Loving is your desire for exclusivity with your partner, the desire to possess, care for, and be with him or her. Consider these statements from the love scale developed by Rubin:

1. If I could never be with my romantic partner, I would feel miserable.
2. If I were lonely, my first thought would be to seek my romantic partner out.
3. I would forgive my romantic partner for practically anything.

Contrast the above points with the three below that seek to measure whether you *like* your romantic partners:

1. I think that my romantic partner is unusually well adjusted.
2. My romantic partner is one of the most likeable people I know.
3. My romantic partner is the sort of person whom I myself would like to be.

In contrast to the first three statements, the latter three attempt to determine if you would care for your partner even if you were not involved with him or her romantically. By using questions from the above liking and loving scales, try to identify your sources of attraction for your current or former romantic partners. Are you mainly attracted because they satisfy your emotional needs, or do you genuinely like them independently of their involvement with you? Would you seek their opinions on an issue important to you even if you did not date them? Do you think they have good judgment, good values, good personality traits? Do you find yourself trying to be more like them? Positive answers to these questions suggest that you like your partners, in addition to whatever other feelings you might have for them.

You may now be asking whether it is more important to like or love a partner. Ideally, it is best that you both like and love your partner. Yet as we have discussed, you may love someone and not really like them. Put another way, you may become involved with a partner you do not like very much, but who, for whatever reasons, satisfies your need to have a partner. This is without a doubt an emotionally hazardous situation, but one you probably have experienced at least once.

I remember an acquaintance named Arlene, a department store sales clerk, who obviously was in love with a man named Bryant. Bryant had a high RMV. He was handsome, had a good newspaper job, and was funnier than Bill Cosby. Yet, Arlene felt that Bryant was shallow and self-centered. For this reason, Arlene did not really like Bryant. She said she had intended to date Bryant for a short time, then move on to someone whom she could not only love but really like. Their relationship dragged on for three years, but Arlene told me she could never make a commitment to him. She finally broke off the relationship. Her only regret is that she spent three precious years with him while her biological clock was ticking away. She promised herself that after that relationship she would never try to force herself to stay with a person she really did not like.

Arlene's situation is one reason why I think that, in the long haul, it is as important to like (and be liked by) your partners as to love them. After all, feelings of love are apt to ebb and flow during the course of romance. Liking your partner can make the relationship more stable, as you stand a better chance of sustaining your relationship when its more romantic aspects falter. Nothing can take the place of liking and being liked by your partner. After all, if you like one another and the relationship doesn't work out, you have a better chance of at least remaining friends and maintaining mutual admiration and respect for each other. Beyond a doubt, then, it is ideal to have all three emotions—like, love, and lust—in your romantic life.

Are There Different Styles Of Loving?

It seems that each of us is inclined to have a different idea of how love should look and feel. This point is evident by the variety of styles of expressing love. These are typically categorized into six unique types:

Eros, or romantic love; *Ludus*, or game-playing love; *Storge*, or friend-ship love; *Mania*, possessive or dependent love; *Pragma*, or logical love; and *Agape*, selfless love. Let's review these styles.

EROS

Lamar is known about town as something of a lady's man. He always looks like he just stepped out of an advertisement in *Ebony Man* or *GQ*. In addition to being very good looking, his physical bearing and grace give him the appearance of a black James Bond, which is why, in fact, his nickname is 007. He is virtually always accompanied by stunning women. It is clear that his dates first and foremost must be beautiful.

Lamar is openly affectionate with women, even those he has just met. It is not uncommon to see him meet a woman at the beginning of a social gathering and be seen kissing her lightly on the cheek or hold-ing her close to him later during the same evening. Lamar is among those individuals whom psychologists classify as *Eros* in their style of love. *Eros* lovers focus heavily on the importance of physical beauty and attractiveness. Like Lamar, most *Eros* lovers are also quick to warm up to their partners and are apt to engage in intimate behaviors quick-ly.

LUDUS

Another dynamic friend of mine is Guy, who sports a heavy mustache, has a six-figure income, and plays as hard as he works. To some he is affectionately known as the "Heartbreak Kid," but his best friend's wife commonly refers to him as "Mr. Trouble," because he is so often in some romantic dilemma. Guy's style of love is game-oriented. For him, love is a fun activity and not to be taken too seriously. Lying and being insincere are justified as part of the nature of romantic involvement. And although there is no intent on Guy's part to hurt his partners, he remorsefully admits that he sometimes does. Guy engages in what psy-chologists refer to as *Ludus* love. This style is often played out with sev-eral romantic partners. *Ludus* lovers are seemingly able to enter in and out of relationships easily. Those who exhibit a *Ludus* style of loving tend also to avoid great emotional involvement. Finally, there is some evidence that Guy is not unique in his style of loving, as men tend to exhibit *Ludus* love styles more than women. I am sure that a lot of brothers hate to admit this, but brothers, the truth is the truth!

STORGE

Mattie is an articulate and soft-spoken social worker who spends much of her time advocating for the educational and economic rights of black children. She admits that for her, love is based on caring and concern. Mattie views love as an extension of friendship. She says that love need not involve heated passion. Instead, she feels love should grow out of concern for her partners. Mattie dates infrequently, but when she does, she is inclined to have rather serious and long-lasting romances. *Storge* lovers like Mattie are not looking for excitement in a relationship. Indeed, they often tend to be shy about physical contact and sexual behavior.

MANIA

Love for Helen, on the other hand, is always hot and heavy, if not high drama. More often than not, her romantic partners are considered heroes one minute and bastards the next. She admits to being preoccupied frequently with thoughts of her partner. She says that some days she cannot seem to get enough of someone she's dating, and experiences an intense desire to see and be with him. Often Helen appears to be out of control emotionally. Much of her time in new relationships seems to be spent trying to force her partners into ever-increasing demonstrations of their love and affection for her. Yet, despite her apparent emotional instability, Helen has little trouble attracting romantic partners—she says that they love the heat she generates. A *Mania* style of loving was best epitomized (to an extreme degree) in the movie *Fatal Attraction*, a most frightening movie for those in the dating scene. This is the kind of love that most of us can readily do without.

PRAGMA

Bobbie is a sales clerk in her late thirties. A Buppie, she is always impeccably dressed and says that she believes in shopping as hard for romantic partners as she does for her clothing. So love for her is unlikely to occur by chance. Bobbie is a *Pragma.* Her motto seems to be, "Romance without finance is a nuisance." She is quick to note that she brings a lot to the romantic table; therefore, she expects a lot from her partner when he sits down. *Pragma* lovers like Bobbie are practical in that they try to find partners who are from good backgrounds, hold good jobs, and make good money, in addition to sharing similar attitudes and interests to themselves.

Bobbie calls herself a romantic realist, and appears to adhere to many of the notions espoused by those who believe in the social-exchange theory of romance. Actually, in this sense, Bobbie is not so unique, as there is some evidence that women are apt to be more *Pragma* in their approach to love than are men.

AGAPE

Agape love can be characterized as unconditional positive regard. It is compassionate first and foremost. This is the kind of love expressed by Jesus Christ, Mahatma Gandhi, and Dr. Martin Luther King, Jr. *Agape* lovers would claim that they use their strength to help their partners through difficult times. The scene in August Wilson's play *Fences* in which the woman, Rose, takes in the baby her husband, Troy, had by another woman while he was still married to Rose, is a case of *Agape* love. Researchers have found no examples of pure *Agape* lovers. But who knows, maybe you will!

In general, black men are apt to be more "erotic" and "ludic" in their styles of loving than are black women. Black women, on the other hand, are likely to be more "pragmatic," "manic," and "storgic" in their romantic styles. However, be careful in applying these classifications to your partners. The classifications are only gross generalizations of types of love. Do not go into the romantic marketplace expecting to find a partner who embodies all the characteristics of any one of these types of love. Indeed, expecting these generalizations to hold true purely on the basis of some isolated action on the part of your partner is likely to short-circuit your romantic involvement.

You may end up promoting stereotypes in your partners. Such love classifications, although potentially helpful to your general understanding of love, may also lead to self-fulfilling prophecies of the worst kind in your dating experiences. The thing to remember is that neither your own romantic behavior nor that of your partner is likely to embody any one of these styles of love. You are instead most likely to find some aspect of each type, both in yourself and in others.

Who Loves First?

Before leaving the subject of love, let me address two frequently asked questions: Are women more likely to fall in love with their partners than men? And for whom, men or women, is the termination of a romance most difficult? Despite the common stereotype of women being more inclined toward romance than men, research suggests that the reverse may be true. It seems that men may adhere more closely to the notion of love at first sight and to the idea that barriers to romantic involvement—such as race, religion, and economics—can be overcome by love. Perhaps equally surprising is the finding that men have been known to rate the desire to fall in love as a significantly more important reason for entering into romantic relationships than women. There is also evidence that men experience greater attraction to their dates sooner than do women.

Men are believed to fall in love sooner because the implications of doing so are less crucial for them. The assumption is that a woman's social and economic status is more dependent on the resources of the man she marries, and that the woman is not only choosing a mate but is determining her future lifestyle. That's why, the argument goes, a woman cannot afford to fall in love without first making an assessment of her partner's value relative to other suitors in the marketplace. Men, it is believed, can afford to be romantic, as they need not be as calculating with respect to a potential mate's social and economic characteristics.

Sociologist Willard Waller wrote in 1938, "There is a difference between men and women in the pattern of bourgeois family life. A man, when he marries, chooses a companion and perhaps a helpmate, but a woman chooses a companion and at the same time a standard of living. It is necessary for a woman to be mercenary." Because women are continuing to make larger contributions to the incomes of their families, however, Waller's observation is less true today, especially for blacks. It follows that black women don't have to take future financial considerations into account as often as they once did in deciding whether to give their heart to a man. Black women may now be willing to fall in love more quickly because of their greater economic security. In other words, many black women perhaps can now better afford to fall in love with their mates early on in their relationships, just as black men have traditionally had the option of doing.

The differences in socialization between men and women is a second explanation as to why women might be less inclined to fall in love early in a relationship. Women, it is believed, are taught to be more socially sensitive than men. For example, women have been found to be better at reading and interpreting the nonverbal communications of others than are men. Hence, women may be both better and more cautious in their evaluations of their romantic partners, and less inclined to make premature judgments about the romantic desirability of their dates.

It also appears that women may be more inclined to terminate their unsatisfactory romantic involvements than are men. Research suggests that women are more inclined than men both to fall out of love, and to break off romantic relationships. It is noteworthy that when a breakup is initiated by men, it is generally because they are the less involved in the relationship. Rarely, it appears, are men inclined to break off relationships when they are the more involved of the two mates. However, women are likely to call it quits even when they are heavily involved in a relationship, if they view the relationship as unworkable. Such scenarios have resulted in women being called "LIFOs"—the "last in, first out" of a relationship. In contrast, men are referred to as "FILOs"—the "first in, last out" of a romance.

Breaking Up Is Hard To Do

As the soul singer Jerry Butler reminded us years ago, "Breaking up is hard to do." Most singles are quick to acknowledge as much. But they often wonder which gender finds romantic breakups most difficult. Actually, it appears that women may be tougher in this respect than men.

Dwayne and Barbara, for example, used to be regarded as one of the happiest couples in a circle of friends I knew. Dwayne, however, is not a detail man, either in his job as a sales manager or in his love life, according to Barbara. "His whole mode of thinking in both cases seemed to be to concentrate on the big picture," she related. "He could walk in the door, give me a kiss, and settle down for dinner without noticing that I was in a bad mood. He seldom asked me how my day went. He assumed that because we were together and I wasn't bitching, everything must be O.K. It was as if he expected problems to work themselves out without much input from him. He concentrated on the big picture, our living together under one roof, but he didn't see the little things that made me miserable. We had arguments about this, but he always said we'd work them out, and then he'd move right back to business as usual. My telling him one evening that I was going to move out of the apartment was a total shock to him."

Dwayne's attitude and behavior is typical of many men. He was less aware of the difficulties in the relationship and was more distressed and taken aback by what appeared to him to be an abrupt decision by Barbara. Like Barbara, women in general seem more likely to sense breakups approaching than men do, and are able to offer more explanations for their occurrence. Consistent with Barbara's observations, it appears that women also experience less emotional strain after the affair is over. They appear to rebound more quickly and may experience fewer hard feelings. Even when a breakup was initiated by their partners, and despite experiencing some unhappiness, women tend to be less inclined to retain the hope that the romantic damage can be repaired, and less likely to regret not giving love one more try.

To Love Or Not To Love

To seek romance is to risk unhappiness. Many of your most unpleasant memories probably have to do with experiencing the heartaches of some flawed love affair. Hence, by increasing the odds of finding romantic partners—which is the foremost goal of this book—you are simultaneously increasing the probabilities of your experiencing romantic disappointment. The fact that you are reading this book, however, suggests that you must have decided that the potential gains are worth the potential risks.

It seems that hard experience has caused some black singles to lose the ability to feel much in the way of love. For them the potential emotional costs have come to outweigh the possible benefits. Such people, we sometimes say, have become jaded, pessimistic, or bitter. They are the casualties of love affairs lost. They have become disillusioned and are no longer willing to experience the lows of love, and their attendant risks, in an attempt to experience the highs.

Black singles in particular are especially weighted down with bad news about romance, such as high divorce rates and poor images of themselves as romantic partners. Some black singles obviously differ in their abilities to withstand the emotional strains of falling in and out of love. This may explain why some of them seek to establish intimate relationships less frequently than do others. In contrast, it appears that some individuals are in and out of intimate relationships all the time and are seemingly no worse for the wear. It could be said that those who suffer most from failed love affairs do so because they love their partners more deeply. It also is possible that people simply handle their experiences differently.

But make no mistake, romance is difficult for everyone. Anyone who is dating is taking a risk. There is no guarantee that our romantic lives will be forever trouble-free. So don't give up on finding love because you've been "burned." Who hasn't been? With a little luck, chances are that you'll find someone who thinks you're great. You're likely to find yourself falling right back in love again—and a little wiser this time around!

13 Sex: When, Why, And With Whom

A S THE SEXUAL STANDARDS of the larger society have changed, so have those of black singles. Take premarital sex, for example. Now glamorized by virtually all forms of media, premarital sex has become far more widespread than it was prior to the 1960s. Gone is the double standard that made it acceptable for men but not women to have sex before marriage.

A majority of black singles now anticipate premarital sex, but men and women differ on the circumstances under which they deem this practice acceptable. Research has consistently shown that men in general are more likely to view having sex as the most important goal in a romantic relationship. Although the number of females who engage in premarital sex is increasing, sex for them clearly continues to be determined by the extent of their emotional attachment to a partner. In other words, they are more likely to have sex with those romantic partners they love, or at least like.

When is the best time in a relationship to begin having sex? Does it matter whether couples have sex sooner rather than later? Does having it either sooner or later affect the quality or duration of a relationship? These questions are frequently debated, even argued about, among black singles. If left up to most men, sex with their partners would begin as soon as possible (call it the "Let's get it on" mentality). Much to the frustration of most men, however, their partners are invariably in less of a hurry to make love. There is, of course, no absolute number of dates or days that must pass before it is O.K. for a couple to engage in sex. The right time varies from couple to couple, but for some unexplained reason, a significant number of sexual relationships tend to start on or around a couple's third date.

Couples who postpone sexual intercourse are likely to include female partners who are more conservative or traditional in their values and behavior. In contrast, couples who have sex early in their relationships, for example, within their first month of dating, are likely to include females partners who are less traditional in their outlooks. These women are also more likely to be less interested in being full-time housewives, and more interested in their careers.

Evidence suggests that whether partners have sex sooner or later, it does not appear to affect how satisfying their romantic relationship is likely to be. Nor does it seem to influence the duration of a relationship. Still, the timing of sex does influence the types of partners we become involved with. Knowing this is potentially useful. For example, it may tell you whether your sexual timing is out of sync with your romantic aspirations. Or it may cause you to attract partners for whom you are not best suited in terms of physical satisfaction as well as moral values.

Women can use this knowledge as a way of screening romantic candidates. They can better weed out those men whose sexual habits are at variance with their own, and screen in those whose outlooks are compatible with theirs. Knowing that a man is in no hurry to have sex may tell you a lot about the man himself. It may suggest, for instance, that he holds many traditional values, which may or may not jibe with your own lifestyle.

An often-asked question is whether someone is appreciated more for insisting that his or her partner wait. There is little to suggest that using sex as a "carrot" per se is likely to promote romance. I know there is evidence that people are inclined to appreciate more those things for which they have worked harder and longer. This rule isn't necessary applicable to sex, however; the people doing the waiting might feel that sex is being used as a ploy, a way to exploit or manipulate them. Many partners dislike viewing sex as a payment for patience. Therefore, it's erroneous to think that postponing sex will increase the extent to which your partner is attracted to you. If you prefer less-traditional romantic partners, the "make them wait" game may cause you to waste time with individuals whom you don't really want, and to lose those who might be more compatible with you.

By the same token, the relative shortage of eligible black men may encourage black women to have sex when they think it is best for the relationship, rather than when they think it's best for them. This is almost always a mistake. You will always do best by following your true feelings and personal comfort levels; have sex when it feels right for you, and not just when you have been asked to have it. This less-calculated approach will create more honest and satisfying relationships, and generate better match-ups between you and partners with compatible values.

Although employing timing as a screening tactic may be less useful for men, they can still benefit from knowing the implications of the timing of sex. Yet men have no indirect way of determining whether a woman is either conservative or liberal in her sexual outlook. Because men are generally expected to initiate sex, they have to either ask for sex, or at least bring up the topic, in order to find out the views of their partners—unless, of course, a man is seduced by his partner. In that case, even males who hold traditional attitudes about sex are likely to agree to engage in sex sooner rather than later. Most men will find it difficult to "Just Say No" to a woman who has just said yes.

Even though men are expected to be the aggressors where sex is concerned, my advice to most men is to ease up a bit. The woman who rejects a sexual advance or two may well be your most compatible romantic partner. Consider the relationship between Charles and Irene.

Charles, who is now a mailman, said he used to think something was wrong with him because his traditional values about sex and women didn't mesh with those of other boys in the Detroit public housing project where he grew up. Charles recalls that his buddies used to fantasize about bedding every pretty woman that crossed their paths, whereas he had been a one-woman man all his life—or wanted to be, until something happened about the time he met Irene.

As he grew older, Charles discovered that many of the women he dated almost assumed that he wasn't monogamous, and expected him to want sex soon after meeting them. He joked that a few of his dates even implied that he was "funny" because he didn't show any immediate interest in sexual intercourse. Charles said he thus began to be more assertive. Then he became interested in Irene, who worked at a convenience store that was on his mail route.

After attending a concert on their first date, the couple returned to Irene's apartment for coffee and dessert. Charles turned on his charm, but found Irene to be more firm than most women in putting off his advances. Thereafter, whenever he called for a date, she accepted with the proviso that sex would not be part of the deal. Charles finally decided to stop calling her, and she began dating another person whom she eventually married.

Charles said it soon dawned on him that he cared deeply for Irene and realized that her traditional attitudes about marriage and sex were congruent with his own latent views about relationships. As a result of attempting to initiate sex sooner rather than later, many other black men commit Charles's error. They chase away some women who are actually better suited for them than some of the women who stay.

Who Should Initiate Sex?

This brings up an interesting question. Should women initiate sex? Those who think not forget that women are increasingly more similar to men in most every respect. They hold important positions of authority throughout society, and many of them now feel assertive enough to initiate sex. That is a totally healthy response, consistent with women's striving toward equality in, and away from, the workplace.

Nevertheless, most black couples are still apt to view the man as the one who should initiate sex. Even though most men are likely to accept a direct request for sex, indications are that such invitations aren't always well received. Some research has found romantic relationships to be less satisfying for both partners in certain cases where sex has been initiated by the female partner.

This observation points to an important aspect in male-female relationships: some of the stated romantic views of men—such as feeling at ease with liberated women—conflict with what their egos can comfortably handle. Clearly, many black men, notwithstanding their macho statements, do not really feel comfortable about being hit on sexually. Romantic assertiveness on the part of the black woman probably robs some black men of their most familiar role of being the romantic aggressor.

Moreover, many black men are likely to be intimidated by women who assume the role of sexual initiator, because they prefer to perceive themselves as being more sexually knowledgeable and experienced than their partners. There is also evidence to suggest that women who either in discussion or by demonstration indicate that they have had greater sexual experience than their partner are likely to be viewed unfavorably by that partner. This attitude is unquestionably a carry-over from the traditional double standard regarding male/female sexual behavior.

Not that being a virgin, or sexually inexperienced, is always a plus. It has been said that most black men would prefer to date Miss New York, while they would rather marry Miss Virginia. Perhaps it's fair to acknowledge that men don't want women they perceive to be more sexually experienced than they, but do feel that it's all right for a partner to have had some experience. It may also be true that many men feel that it's O.K. to fool around with a more experienced woman, but would prefer to have as "their woman" one who is less experienced. It seems wise, then, for black women to assess the sexual experience of their partners prior to divulging their own—and even then, to let the male believe that he has had more experiences than they. To play it safe, about all a woman should admit to is that she isn't a virgin. Despite the sexual revolution and the liberation of women, things haven't really changed that much in the minds (and egos) of black men!

At the same time, it's best for black men to go slow in recounting their own previous exploits. While women are probably better at accepting the fact that their partners have had a greater number of sexual experiences than they, nobody wants someone who has "done everything with everybody"—and insists on bragging about it. Furthermore, recounting earlier sexual exploits may come back to haunt either partner in some later discussion or argument about loyalty or sexual promiscuity.

Infidelity: The Extra Sexual Partner

Pick up any weekly tabloid, listen to any blues song, or watch any daily soap opera and you'll find that the issue of infidelity jumps out at you. In fact, one of the most consistent sources of romantic problems is the "other" woman or man.

It is common to hear black women state that black men won't commit themselves to monogamous relationships. What's the deal here? Why does it seem that so many black men have more than one sexual partner? The shortage of black men means that black men have more potential partners to choose from than do black women. It should be made clear, however, that "extra" sexual affairs are not unique to black people, but are common among all ethnic groups. Black couples should attempt to keep this point in mind, since they are often portrayed as being oversexed and less faithful than the rest of the population—so much so that they run the risk of believing such negative stereotypes about themselves.

An attractive nursing student once asked me how she could get her boyfriend to break the habit of having more than one sex partner. Innumerable psychologists have been asked the same question and have tried in earnest to answer it. The incidence of such extra sexual relationships remains high, but it appears to be lessening, perhaps primarily in response to the fear of AIDS.

Even though there is no sure way to stop your romantic partner from having sex with others, understanding the common sources of this behavior may help. For example, you might conclude that partners who engage in extra sexual relationships are just plain sick. Many psychologists are more than happy to offer elaborate explanations bolstering this possibility. But extra sexual relationships occur with such frequency as to make them almost the rule rather than the exception. That's why I strongly disagree with those who look for pathological answers to a behavior that is so pervasive: rarely is a phenomenon that is so prevalent throughout whole cultures, races, or classes of people pathological.

Just for a moment, let's ask the obverse question: why *don't* some men or women have extra sexual relationships? The general assumption seems to be that those who don't are the truly decent and committed men and women—obviously in many instances this is true. It is also possible that other factors contribute to their apparent good behavior: they may be less interested in sex; they may be less desirable to others; they may have too little opportunity; or they may simply have already gone through a period of "sexual exploration" and have now turned their efforts and energies to family, civic, or professional pursuits, which also leaves them with less time to be promiscuous. What you may find out about yourself and your partner by considering some of the above points is that, in general, people who have a low probability of engaging in extra sexual affairs may be less interesting or desirable to you, as well as to others. Good-looking women and men tend to attract partners easily. In that sense, you too are more likely to be attracted to a partner who is also attractive to others, and hence is a more likely candidate for an extra sexual affair. Actually there is evidence that individuals who are more attractive, make more money, and are more successful are less likely to be faithful to their partners than those who are less attractive and successful.

In your efforts to find romantic partners who would never have an extra sexual relationship, you may be writing off almost everyone whom you would find romantically interesting or attractive. In short, you may find yourself "cutting off your nose to spite your face." Not only is that unappealing partner unlikely to sleep with anyone besides you, but you may find that you don't want to sleep with that partner for the same reasons others don't—he or she doesn't turn you on.

Engaging in extra sexual relationships, once thought to be primarily a masculine behavior (if not a privilege), is now recognized as being prevalent among both males and females. Most of what we know about extra sexual affairs comes from the data on married couples. Yet it seems reasonable to assume that if people are willing to violate the marriage vows, then the number of extra sexual affairs in dating relationships must be even higher. In 1953, American society was startled by the Kinsey report, which indicated that, by age forty, approximately 50 percent of married men and 25 percent of married women had engaged in extra-marital affairs. Current indications are that the level of extra-marital affairs may be decreasing. But there are also indications that the rate of extra-marital affairs among women is catching up with that of men.

Let me state here that I am not saying that having multiple sex partners is either healthy or desirable. Nor do I wish to encourage this practice among black singles. But I am saying that the "other" man or woman syndrome is so common that those who are really interested in affecting the "extra" sexual behavior of their partners must understand better the motives for this behavior. Don't immediately classify your unfaithful partner as having some weird pathological personality disorder; such labeling will rarely offer you any help. Rather, ask your partners for their personal motives for engaging in sex outside of your relationship. Go ahead! Ask them if they are going to continue sleeping with others, or whether it is a thing of the past, and if so, why?

The answers you receive to these questions may be useful. For example, a partner's reasons for having multiple sex partners may differ considerably from the motives you had anticipated. Once you have identified the possible reasons, you are then better prepared to cope with them. Notice that I didn't say you will be able to stop the practice; only your partner has the power to do that. Of course, you have the option of breaking off the relationship. But the odds are better than fifty-fifty that you'll only wind up with someone else who engages in extra sexual affairs, and whom, in some respects, you may like less than your old partner.

My advice is to hang in there (at least for a while) and attempt to undermine the source of the problem. You may find that you can provide what your partner is attempting to find outside of your relationship. But you first must determine what you're up against—you must identify and talk about what is driving your partner's desire for sex with others. As with married couples, the incidence of extra sexual relationships among single couples is likely to be influenced by a variety of factors: the desire for sexual novelty, opportunity, romantic dissatisfaction, or even revenge ("spite sex"). Let's quickly review some of these common motives for engaging in extra sexual relationships.

Joe, a small, dark-skinned man who is a regular customer at my brother's barber shop, would often say—when the topic of discussion turned to sex—that his girlfriend "could give me some *more* sex, but not any *new* sex." Such a rationale for seeking new sexual partners is probably not limited to Joe. Clearly, new and varied sexual experiences must be highly desirable, since so many people engage in them despite their potential for ruining reputations, fortunes, families, and careers, not to mention relationships.

The desire for sexual novelty is, I believe, the greatest single factor that leads to extra sexual relationships for men. Put simply, many men find the idea of new sexual partners exciting. For men, it is probably the case that most extra sexual affairs are more sexual than romantic. It also is probably true that many of those who engage in such affairs for the purposes of sex are forced to sustain a facade of romance, because otherwise their extra sexual partners are unlikely to comply with their sexual advances.

In contrast to the motives of men, women are more likely to have a stronger emotional motivation for pursuing extra sexual relationships. In fact, sex is often only a by-product of the satisfaction of some other need, e.g., a desire for intimacy. But here, too, attitudes and behaviors are changing. Black women, like other women, are becoming more like men, by "unlearning" the expectation of emotional involvement in order to go to bed with a desirable sexual partner.

Opportunity—in terms of the availability of alternative sexual partners—is a critical factor affecting romantic commitment. The fact that black men have so many more potential sexual partners available to them than do black women increases the probability that black men will have more extra sexual relationships. Because the numbers are so skewed in favor of black men, it has been suggested that black women should simply engage in "man sharing." This strategy would have the benefit of reducing the frequency of conflicts resulting from the deceit in extra sexual relationships. However, the sharing of partners is unlikely to occur in a formal way, since most black men and women are too jealous to accept openly the fact that their partner is sleeping with someone else.

Men also have greater sexual opportunity because of their traditionally greater mobility in the workplace. But in this respect, the opportunities for women to have extra sexual relationships is increasing. As women have been liberated from the home and child care in increasing numbers, and have created their own sources of income, their sexual behavior has more closely resembled that of men. It has been known for some time that men who earn more money are more likely to have extra sexual relationships. It should come as no surprise that the rising income and professional mobility of women will also bring increasing instances of extra sexual affairs.

Dissatisfaction is also a big contributor to sexual infidelity. Many singles are romantically shopping around for that exciting and special person, someone who is unlike all the other people they've dated. One thing each new partner offers is hope: hope that the new person will be Mr. or Ms. Right—a great lover, good looking, brilliant, kind, romantic. This search leads some singles to sleep around—holding on to what they have, while looking around for what they want. It is possible that once these singles find someone who closely fits their romantic ideal, they will become sexually committed to that partner. It is also possible that their romantic criteria are so stringent that no one partner will ever measure up to their romantic expectations.

It is also possible that sex itself is the problem. If so, you might want to work on ways to improve that aspect of your relationship. Despite the comments of those who speak to the contrary, sex is very important to romantic relationships. Any marriage counselor will readily tell you that sex and money are the two most common things over which couples fight. Having a satisfying sexual relationship is perhaps the best offense against needing a defense against sexual infidelity. So attempt to be good at sex! Ask for feedback from your partner as to how you can make sex with him or her better. I am convinced that those who are good sexual partners have an excellent chance of sustaining romance, and reducing the probability that their partners will seek sex elsewhere. I have for years recommended to my colleagues and friends that if they want to brush up on their sexual knowledge and skills, they should purchase what is now an old book, *The Sensuous Woman*, and completely review it with their partners. It is rather graphic, and may make some of you blush, but then perhaps that's a good place to start.

Finally, our partners may elect to engage in an extra sexual relationship as a means of "getting even." Most often I have heard of women more than men employing this as a rationale for having extra sexual relationships. It seems that such situations are most likely to occur as a result of the man first having had sex outside the relationship, and the woman taking on a lover in retaliation. This well-known phenomenon is commonly referred to as "spite sex." Both men and women probably engage in the practice in order to strike back at their romantic partners. Very often the recipients of "spite sex" are the other partner's social, political, or economic rivals.

Whatever the reason for your partner's extra sexual affair, it is important for you to attempt to understand it. Don't automatically assume, however, that the affair means something is wrong with you. Before assuming that it is a reflection of an unmet need, you should first inspect the extra sexual relationship for what it very likely is—sex and not love. In either event, once facing up to the issue and its ramifications, you will be better able to determine what course of action you should take.

You, Your Partner, And AIDS

AIDS has made dating a risky business. One of the big questions asked by singles—should I limit my sexual activities to a single partner?—takes on even greater significance in light of the prevalence of sexually transmitted diseases, particularly AIDS. There are sensible ways to broach this unpleasant and difficult topic with new partners. While a discussion about AIDS is not a very romantic one, it will increase your probabilities of sustaining both life and romance in the 1990s.

Because he seemed so invincible, the disclosures by Magic Johnson substantially heightened the fear of contracting AIDS among black singles. In fact, Magic Johnson testing HIV-positive struck fear in the hearts of most black singles, and for good reason: blacks account for 30 percent of all reported AIDS cases in the United States, and black females account for 52 percent of all American women with the disease. Although most AIDS cases are attributed to intravenous drug use and homosexuality, the fastest rate of AIDS growth is now among heterosexuals, and particularly heterosexual black women.

There are a number of measures you might employ to reduce your chances of contracting AIDS. The most effective is to stop having sex. Clearly while this is the most fool-proof way to avoid contracting AIDS, most of us are unlikely to follow it. It is believed that some who do attempt this strategy engage in a form of diet/binge behavior. That is, they don't have sex with anyone for a period of time, and then they fall off the wagon, so to speak, and begin having sex again, often unprotected.

On the other hand, sexual exclusivity is more likely to be adhered to than abstinence. Find someone and limit your sexual activity to him or her. This is probably the most commonly attempted method that singles employ in their efforts to protect themselves. The major problem with this method is that sexual exclusivity is a form of commitment, and generally occurs after a period of time following a couple's first sexual contact. Hence considerable time (and opportunities at other sexual relationships) is likely to pass before you and your partner make such an agreement. To be effective, both you and your partner should be tested for AIDS before having sex, and then enter into a vow of sexual exclusivity.

Try to engage in sexual acts with lower probabilities of exposing you to the AIDS virus. For example, you may want to try engaging in mutual masturbation. This can be done manually or with technological assistance. Mutual masturbation will allow both you and your partner to reach sexual orgasm but not exchange body fluids that might potentially expose you to the AIDS virus. Actually, this strategy is an excellent one for getting yourself out of intense erotic situations. Finally, cease engaging in anal sex, with or without a condom; rubbers do break, and anal sex is known to be one of the most frequent methods of AIDS transmission.

Always use condoms if you plan to have any type of sexual intercourse. Cease having vaginal or oral sex without using a condom. Wearing condoms also reduces your risk of contracting gonorrhea, syphilis, herpes, and chlamydia. There is little doubt that this is the AIDS prevention method of choice. Even if you later plan to establish an exclusive sexual relationship with your partner, start off using condoms. If things work out between the two of you and you decide to become each other's only lover, then you can always consider other options.

However you do it, you should cut down on the number of your sexual partners. In this case, the more is not the merrier. Cease having sex with people you don't know well, and with those whom you know to have several other sex partners. Don't sleep with everyone you date. Be more discriminating—decide that some of those you date will be partners with whom you go to the movies or out to dinner, but not to bed.

Just another comment here on reducing your odds of contracting AIDS—avoid "risky partners." While it is not possible to determine who has AIDS just by looking at them, some groups of individuals should raise your red flag. These people are known to have the highest rates of AIDS, and you should make a concerted effort to avoid sexual contact with them. For example, bisexual men; men or women who "shoot" drugs or who have done so in the past; drug dealers, as they may trade drugs for sex with high-risk persons; male or female prostitutes and their sex partners. Indeed having sex with prostitutes is especially risky, as an alarming number of prostitutes in the major urban areas, such as New York, Chicago, Los Angeles, Washington, and Detroit have tested positive for exposure to the AIDS virus.

Discussing AIDS With Your Partner

Somebody once said anything done in excess is harmful, including moderation. The sexual revolution seemed to have been based on that proposition. The guiding principle was: If it feels good, do it, and as often as possible. However, the no-holds-barred sexual behavior that was so common in the sixties and seventies is now giving way to restraint. It wouldn't hurt if every father warned his son not to allow the little head (the penis) to think for the big head (the brain). Girls, too, need to be reminded of the need for discretion.

People need to find ways to avoid allowing sexual arousal to get in the way of common-sense precautions. Suppose you meet the person you are certain is the man or woman of your dreams. You have been meaning to have a discussion with that person about AIDS. But before you do—bang!—you find yourself in a compromising position. The logical thing to do at that point is to stand up, compose yourself, and go home. Call the person later and have a discussion about AIDS. Failing that, here are some suggestions you might want to employ.

Women, try telling your partner that you are not on the pill and that you always use condoms. Or tell your partner straight out: "no glove, no love." This strategy will allow you more time to assess the risk factors of your partner. You'll also feel better if your romance turns out to be a brief one, as you have expended very little effort and gained the benefit of protecting your health.

It was suggested in a recent U.S. Surgeon General's message on AIDS that if you know someone well enough to have sex, then you should be able to talk to them about AIDS. While this assumption seems quite reasonable, it is probably frequently not true. A discussion about AIDS between dating partners, like a discussion about birth control, has a good probability of occurring after sexual intercourse rather than before it. This is true foremost because romantic couples like to think of a first sexual encounter as a spontaneous act—something neither partner had planned, but rather something that just happened.

Furthermore, some black women may be reluctant to initiate a discussion of AIDS with partners with whom they are not yet sexually involved, for fear that such a discussion will make them appear sexually aggressive, or that it will in some way serve to commit them to having sex afterwards. Indeed, both men and women may hesitate to initiate a discussion on AIDS, for fear that it might suggest they are infected or that they are in some way suggesting that the person with whom they are having the discussion might be infected.

So starting a conversation on AIDS is frequently a difficult aspect of AIDS prevention for many black singles. It is with this fact in mind that I offer some simple but helpful strategies for initiating such a discussion.

First, you should be prepared to be assertive. You should get in the habit of introducing a discussion about AIDS with everyone you even remotely think you might have sex with. Your introduction of a discussion on AIDS with your new date should occur in an easy, calm, nonjudgmental manner. You are attempting to find out if your new date is a high-risk person for contracting AIDS, to what extent he or she has or is currently engaging in high-risk AIDS behaviors, and to what extent he or she practices safe sex.

The following are some possible lead-in questions:

1) "Did you see that TV documentary on AIDS. It's really something, isn't it? So many people are dying from it. It has certainly affected me. The documentary pointed out that only famous people get attention for dying of AIDS, but a lot more not-so-famous people also have died of AIDS (list some by name if you know any; if you don't, make some up). Do you know anyone who has died of AIDS?"

2) "Besides probably scaring the hell out of you, how has the fear of catching AIDS affected your sexual behavior?"

3) "What are you doing to protect yourself and your partner(s) from catching AIDS?" (Here's a chance to say what you are doing, too.)

Some Final Words On Condoms And Their Use

Begin using condoms immediately. It is probably harder to go from not using condoms to using condoms with a given partner. So, begin any new sexual relationships by using condoms from the start. If you fail to use condoms the first time you have sex with a new partner, use them for sure the next time. Most people are inclined to think that if they didn't use condoms the first time, then it's too late to start. Their logic goes something like this: If my partner has AIDS, now I have it too; so why use condoms now? If my partner doesn't have AIDS, then why use condoms at all? This reasoning seems logical, but it happens to be inaccurate. It is possible to have sex with someone who has been infected with the AIDS virus and not get infected yourself. But each time you have sex with that person, you increase your chances of being infected with AIDS. The point is that if you have had sex with a partner while being unprotected, don't assume that it is too late to protect yourself from that partner now—it's not.

Use only latex (rubber) condoms. This is apt to be one of the few instances in your life where the most expensive protection is not the best; the most expensive condoms, those made of animal membranes (generally lamb skin), are thought to be ineffective at stopping the transmission of the AIDS virus. Second, condoms should be used only once. Finally, don't use petroleum products (baby oils, Vaseline, et cetera) to lubricate condoms, as the oil causes the rubber to disintegrate—instead use KY Jelly or a water-based lubricant, or purchase condoms that come already lubricated.

The AIDS epidemic has dramatic implications for sexually active black singles, though there always has been concern among those who date about the possibility of contracting venereal diseases. Typically, contracting a venereal disease meant gonorrhea or syphilis. Few would argue that these are not terrible diseases, but in most instances, they can be cured. However, with the arrival of herpes and AIDS, we are playing, so to speak, a whole new ball game. Indeed, it has been suggested that AIDS has brought the sexual revolution to a close.

14 Dating White

T HE ISSUE OF BLACK-WHITE ROMANCE is often blown out of perspective. This topic, I fear, frequently receives attention beyond its actual significance to black people. It also reduces the amount of time that should be spent focusing on the most significant aspect of black singles life, which is black-on-black romance. In both absolute and relative terms, the number of individuals who are dating white at any given time is small, and there is an extremely low rate of interracial marriages (less than 4 percent). Indeed, blacks have the lowest interracial marriage rate of any nonwhite group. Hispanics have an interracial marriage rate of approximately 40 percent, and for Asians it is estimated to be as high as 60 percent. Somewhat more than half of Native Americans are believed to marry whites. In the scheme of things, interracial romance is for blacks an infrequent event.

Yet in light of the competitiveness of the black romantic marketplace, the concerns frequently expressed by many blacks regarding interracial dating are understandable. Unquestionably, black women are faced with very limited romantic possibilities. In the age bracket spanning from eighteen years to forty-four years, there are only between seven and eight black men for every ten black women. And, as pointed out by the distinguished scholar Robert Staples, considerably more black heterosexual men are lost to prison, drugs, and death than are "lost" to white partners. It is also true that the number of black people who are unemployed reduces the number of eligible black partners far more than does the small number who pair off with whites. For most blacks and whites, the societal prohibitions on interracial dating are often too great to risk starting a relationship. So those blacks who do it must perceive the gains of dating white to outweigh the costs. Even then, as the percentage of blacks who date white is considerably larger than the percentage who marry white, we can only assume that what may be perceived to be a "good deal" in a dating relationship is perceived to be less of a "good deal" in marriage.

Given these realities, it would be a better use of the time we spend thinking about interracial dating to instead create greater life opportunities for black people, and to expand our notions of the "acceptable" black partner. In other words, we should attempt to enlarge the pool of eligible black romantic candidates, rather than spend our time angrily lamenting the very few black men or women who "got away."

Finally, it is easy to say that blacks should date their own kind—but many who take this position are fortunate to have already found partners, or have given up on finding one. Although I will not say that you should or should not date someone who is white, I will say that if you do elect to date white, select a white partner who is of equal RMV to yourself. As the expression goes, "Don't date someone just because they're white."

Why They Do It

Jeanne, a very attractive junior college teacher who grew up in Ann Arbor, Michigan, began dating white men exclusively while completing her studies in American literature at the University of Michigan. Her dates have included a wide assortment of men. Some, like red-haired Harry, have been quite attractive. But others were, by anybody's standards, unattractive. Yet Jeanne seems to find something likeable about all of her white dates.

This nation has been a racial melting pot for many ethnic groups, but the sight of Jeanne and other black people who elect to date whites still tends to turn heads and generate anxiety among many onlookers. Interracial dating continues to be a focus for social scientists, and a hot topic among talk show hosts, mainly because no other topic so inflames the emotions of both blacks and whites. Unquestionably, the most efficient way to destroy the positive ambiance of a good party or evening's discussion is to initiate a conversation on black-white dating. Following the introduction of this topic, an evening has a good probability of becoming an emotional brawl. The reaction is not surprising, since the topic of black-white romance combines two very emotionally potent issues—sex and racism.

But talk about black-white dating isn't limited to dinner parties. Janice, former president of the local AKA sorority, mentioned to me that the issue of "jungle fever" continues to be a hot topic at the group's monthly meetings. I got an earful about how strongly some of her sisters feel about this issue. Janice related that she and a friend, Diane, were eating a snack at an outdoor cafe when a black man and white woman strode by their table ("The third such couple in about twenty minutes," she said with a frown). Janice said her friend quipped, "Now I know why I spend Friday nights talking on the phone with friends. All the brothers are busy dating white girls." Janice added that she and Diane later left the cafe and hadn't walked more than a block before they stopped to chat with two black male acquaintances. At that point, she said, a female TV newscaster, who happened to be black, strolled by with a white professional football player, holding hands. After the couple passed, Janice related that one of the normally apolitical black men got serious and sarcastic for a minute, saying, "Wow! Another sister with a white boy. Man, I'm telling you, these sisters here are going white-boy crazy!"

Concerns about interracial dating are commonly expressed by both black men and women, although typically it has been white men and black women who have most vehemently expressed their opposition to interracial romance. This is understandable, as they have perceived themselves as having the most to lose, because white women and black men have thus far been the principal interracial partners on the black-white dating scene. But as we shall discuss later, things may be changing.

There is, of course, no single reason why blacks become romantically involved with whites. However, from the perspective of many blacks, motives having to do with self-hatred have been by far the most common explanation. They generally hold that those who date or marry non-blacks are often rebelling either against themselves, society, or both. Perhaps the most common explanation contends that those who break America's strongest racial taboos by engaging in interracial romance must be experiencing psychological difficulties. By dating white, the blacks are said to have renounced their racial group. There are no data available to inform us as to what proportion (if any) of blacks who date whites fall into this category. However, there are indications that some do. In any event, many who engage in interracial dating do appear to prefer very limited and generally superficial contact with members of their own race; not only are their romantic partners white, but their friends and associates are also generally white.

That's true of Jack, a strikingly handsome, light-skinned brother who earns his living as a radio DJ. He has been dating white women exclusively for about ten years. He was once engaged to a moderately attractive blond named Donna, a clerk in the office building next to the radio station. Although the engagement didn't work out, Jack told me that he liked Donna's family and friends and that they all accepted him. Jack has always felt comfortable among whites. When in college, for example, he pledged a white fraternity, and he continues to maintain close ties with white male friends. He said that blacks seem uncomfortable around his white buddies and girlfriends; consequently, most of his time is spent with whites.

The social behavior of blacks like Jeanne and Jack lend support to the argument that some blacks who date whites may be experiencing difficulty with their racial identities. These blacks seems to experience greater comfort in the presence of whites, and hence choose to spend the bulk of their free time with them.

Others who date white are thought to be merely experimenting—tasting the forbidden fruit. The course of their interracial dating experiences may be quite brief, once the novelty wears off. Basically, these people are attempting to answer the often-asked question, "Is there a difference?" They are curious about the racial myths surrounding black-white sex.

Some blacks may view interracial dating as a means to enhance their social status. In other words, because whites are in the majority, they are ascribed a higher social status than blacks, and subsequently some blacks may feel that their own status or prestige is enhanced by dating whites. It is interesting to note that dating individuals who belong to the ruling or racial conquering class is neither a new phenomenon, nor one unique to African-Americans. There is precedent to suggest that people have commonly romanced their colonizers and rulers as a means to enhance their own social status. Dating white today, though, may bring less perceived social status to those blacks who do it than it might have in the past. This is in part due to the fact that many of the trend-setters for Black America, who are now accomplished writers, filmmakers, political leaders, et cetera, were active participants in pro-black movements in the sixties and seventies, and are still currently opposed (or are at best neutral) to the idea of black-white romance.

Still others, it seems, date whites as an act of rebellion, a means of striking back at white society for the racism and discrimination they have experienced. Take the case of Eli. If you didn't know better, you'd think this tall, dark-skinned brother who carries himself with such grace is from some place in East Africa. He seems to encourage this identification by wearing African garb. Like Jack, Eli dates white women exclusively. At the same time, he doesn't seem to get emotionally involved with any of them. Furthermore, unlike Jack, he appears to have a great deal of racial pride. He is quick to make pro-black statements and anti-white ones, support black causes, and pick fights with white men. Were it not for the fact that Eli dates white women, we would probably think he was very prejudiced against all white people. Sound confusing? It is. Probably not even Eli really knows for sure why he continues to date white women, and yet appears to dislike white people in general. Perhaps he does it for the reasons some have suggested—to get back at white society.

Perceiving A Better Deal

As was true for the group of black women who discuss interracial dating in the movie *Jungle Fever*, feelings on the topic are varied and extreme. For example, get a group of black men or women together, bring up the subject of interracial dating, and you're likely to hear some pretty strong—and sometimes clearly anti-black—statements, such as:

"White women take better care of you."

"Yeah, man, and they don't give you hassles all the time, like sisters!"

"White men are gentlemen, they are more courteous and kinder than black men. Some black men won't even open a door for you."

"You got that right, sister."

Comments such as these affirm a common explanation that blacks often give for dating whites: they feel they are treated better by their white partners. In this sense, their selection of romantic partners has less to do with race than with obtaining what they perceive to be the best available romantic partner. However, obtaining a "good deal" in the interracial romantic market is often more complex than doing so within one's own racial group. Two factors contribute to this difficulty: black-white differences in social and economic status, and black-white differences in standards of physical attractiveness.

First, because whites are generally ascribed a higher social status than blacks in American society, the black partner is often required to bring more to the relationship than the white partner (i.e., have a higher RMV) in order to compensate for his or her lower social status. Neither partner is likely to verbalize this point, but it is in fact an unspoken trade-off that occurs frequently in many interracial romances. We see evidence of this when a wealthy black entertainer or athlete dates or marries a white. The white partner may also have achieved a high social or professional status—he or she may even be wealthy—but the white partner is most often not an equal with respect to the professional achievements or notoriety of the black partner.

A Hollywood example of this occurred in the movie *Guess Who's Coming to Dinner?* Sidney Poitier played the role of a "super-black"—a medical doctor—while his white girlfriend was average at best. It seems that he was required to have exceptional professional credentials in order to compensate for being black, and hence having lower social status. Many blacks look unfavorably upon what they perceive to be unfair romantic deals of this kind. Such unfair exchanges, they argue, connote acceptance of the white ascription of blacks to inferior social rank. These blacks are angered not so much by the interracial union itself, but by the apparent willingness of blacks to accept white romantic partners who are not their romantic equals. These black onlookers feel that unequal romantic deals reflect poorly on all black people by suggesting that whites are more valuable than blacks.

Whether those individuals who are involved in interracial relationships perceive themselves to have made poor romantic exchanges is another thing. Many blacks who prefer interracial romance adamantly deny that they end up dating whites who are less romantically desirable than themselves. However, their behavior often suggests otherwise. Take the case of Eddie. A forty-year-old black postal worker, Eddie could easily pass for thirty. He calls himself an equal opportunity dater, although the black women seen in his company are noticeably more desirable as romantic partners than his white dates: typically, the white women are much older and generally less attractive. His black dates seem to dress better, are less likely to be overweight, and are more socially sophisticated. Although Eddie says he hasn't thought much about why he dates white women, one gets the feeling from his conversation that he is simply unwilling to confront this aspect of his dating behavior.

In addition to the social status of blacks and whites, differences in their economic standing also contribute to making a fair black-white romantic deal more difficult to obtain. You, no doubt, have heard your share of black reactions to interracial dating. Typically, a black onlooker might ask, "Why is he (or she) dating that white person? She's nothing special; she's just an average white person."

Often white romantic partners are exactly that—just average. In this sense, whites have an advantage in that what society deems average is determined by what is most common among whites. For example, with respect to economic status (income, education, or occupation) what is considered to be average for blacks and whites differs considerably. Consider for a moment that the median income for a white male worker is approximately $27,000. In contrast, the median income for a black male worker is approximately $19,000. Hence, a black man who makes an income of $28,000 is in fact not very average at all—in his peer group he has perhaps an upper middle income. Such differences in the incomes and educational or occupational levels of blacks and whites influence their relative RMVs. In our example here, a black person who earns $28,000 holds a higher economic status position in his or her racial peer group than does the white person in his or her racial peer group. The black person is comparatively "less average," and therefore valued more greatly within the black romantic market. I should also add that as a consequence of the black partner's relative greater value, he or she is a greater "loss" to the black romantic market than is the white partner to the white romantic market.

Finally, American standards of beauty are largely determined by white Americans, and this is reinforced and supported by the media. Whites come closer than blacks to measuring up to these media images of what is considered beautiful. Take a look at an advertisement featuring white models, who may have green eyes and blond hair. It is true that most whites lack these features, but these models do largely resemble the average white. On the other hand, most black models—especially those with green eyes and blond hair—do not even remotely resemble the average black.

Our standards of beauty, even though we may attempt to resist them, are influenced significantly by the majority culture—or what is most typical for white Americans. It is clear, however, that fewer and fewer blacks are continuing to judge themselves by white standards of beauty. Still, the average-looking white, more so than the average-looking black, is likely to be considered to have more desirable physical features. This fact explains why the images in many advertisements often suggest that a black person who is considered attractive must look more like the average white than like the average black.

Thus, by dating white, blacks may perceive themselves to be increasing their probability of getting a more desirable romantic partner. Because of the relative greater numbers of whites who are "average," it may be easier to locate these partners. By including whites into their pool of romantic eligibles, blacks may increase their chances of finding romantic partners they view as attractive, yet whose attributes are less commonly found within the black population. Furthermore, because of the larger pool of white candidates who can be considered "average," black singles may find acquiring "typical" white partners to be easier than obtaining "atypical" black ones.

It seems that blacks who date whites may be inclined to seek partners who are *commonly* found within the white romantic market, and partners who are *less common* to the black romantic market. Due to the likelihood of lesser competition from the white romantic marketplace for these "common" partners, the average white partner may make fewer interpersonal demands on his or her partner than would the "uncommon" black romantic partner. Because of this the white partner may be "easier to keep." That is, the more commonly found white partner may expect less in the way of attention and effort exerted by his or her partners to maintain the relationship, and may therefore also be inclined to put up with more from those partners. This is perhaps the source of such comments often made by black singles, to the effect that white dates are more giving, less demanding, and generally easier to get along with than black ones. Despite the difficulties we have outlined, not all black interracial relationships are inequitable. Some blacks who date white do not perceive themselves, nor are they perceived by most others, as making bad romantic choices.

Eric, thirty-eight years old, is a very attractive, tall, and well-built brother. Pam is a very good-looking white woman in her mid-thirties who has been known to stop traffic in her leather pants. Both are lawyers, both have been married before, and both have kids. They now date each other exclusively. Both Eric and Pam are pursued by other would-be partners, black and white. Eric and Pam say that in the past they both had social and political reasons for electing not to date across the color line; however, each says that when they saw the other, they were simply presented with a romantic deal they couldn't refuse. They just seemed to hit it off right away. While both stated that they used to be concerned with the issues that complicate interracial dating, they said that they now no longer think about them.

Why Do Black Men Do It More?

Tom and Calvin, two high school teachers, were standing outside a popular restaurant when out came a white woman with flaming red hair who was accompanied by one of the city's prominent black lawyers. Calvin turned to Tom and said, "Another brother with a white girl. What's the deal with all this interracial dating anyway? It seems like half the brothers I know are dating white." Such conversations between friends like Tom and Calvin are common. The sighting of interracial couples frequently results in someone asking the question, "Why do black men appear to do it more?"

Actually, black men *do* do it more. Limited data that exist on black interracial dating suggest that black males are approximately three times as likely to date white as are black females. The black interracial marriage rates show a similar high ratio of males over females. It is, however, worth noting that the percentage of blacks who date white is dramatically greater than those who marry white. It is also likely that black men date white for longer periods of time than do black women because they may view themselves as having a longer period before which they must settle down. It is probably the case that a great deal of interracial dating occurs among people who are not looking for a serious relationship, but are instead looking for excitement, a change of pace, or merely sowing wild oats. Their situations may be characterized as the "wrong person-wrong time" scenario we discussed in Chapter Six. It is probably also true that as the "right time" approaches, both black and white singles will increasingly date same-race partners—in other words, "they'll come home."

What accounts for the differences in the ratios of black men and black women who date white? There seem to be two major reasons for this disparity. First, it is important to remember that men and women typically exercise different roles in romantic relationships. Men tend to be the initiators of romance: they typically are the pursuers and women the pursued. Because of this cultural expectation, black men have probably found it easier to broaden their pool of eligibles to include white partners than have black women.

Secondly, as we noted earlier in Chapter Four, the factors of physical attractiveness and status figure significantly more in the romantic selections of men than those of women. Because black women have traditionally been perceived as less attractive according to white standards of beauty, they have been less attractive to white men as sex symbols. In addition, because they belong to an oppressed non-white group, they have also been ascribed a lower social status. Therefore, dating black women has not had the perceived social benefits to white men that dating white women has had for black men, unless they were famous actresses, entertainers, exceptionally beautiful, wealthy, or all of the above.

Are Black Women Catching Up?

Recently I overheard Stan, a barber shop owner, say to Charles, who works for him, "Hey, man, they're taking our women." "Yeah," said Charles, "a lot of the sisters who are into something are dating white guys now."

Trina and Phyllis, both secretaries for a large hospital, discussed this issue with me over lunch. Following a lengthy and at times heated discussion on the pros and cons of dating white, Phyllis concluded by saying to Trina, "It's the in thing today, honey, we better get ourselves some white men to date."

As I mentioned earlier, interracial romance has been an activity engaged in principally by black men and white women, but it seems that things are changing. Both of the conversations above illustrated what appears to be a growing phenomenon—black women dating white men. Anyone who has recently walked down a city street in a major metropolitan area has noted the more-frequent pairings of black females with white males. This change in the gender makeup of the black-white dating scene has received considerable attention in most of the monthly black magazines, and from most black men. A number of factors are contributing to this new interracial reality. Let's look at what appear to be some of the major contributing factors to this new romantic configuration.

- BLACK WOMEN ARE FACED WITH A TERRIBLE ROMANTIC MARKET

First, because of the black-male shortage, many black women are faced with a terrible romantic market. As a result, black women may now be more accepting of the advances of white men, and they may also be more assertive in their own romantic advances toward white men. Secondly, many white men are intensifying their efforts to attract black women.

191

• BLACK HAS BECOME INCREASINGLY BEAUTIFUL

Probably as a direct consequence of the "black is beautiful" consciousness movement begun in the 1960s, white men are increasingly recognizing the beauty of black women. This is perhaps most evident from the recent selection of several Miss Americas who were black.

• BLACKS HAVE BECOME INCREASINGLY MORE WEALTHY AND EDUCATED

White men have not been oblivious to the social advances of black women. The advances brought on by affirmative action programs and the women's movement have enhanced the economic and professional status of black women considerably. These advances have unquestionably raised the RMV levels of black females, and made them more desirable as romantic partners.

• INCREASED INTERACTION AS EQUALS

In altering their social status, black women have also altered the conditions under which much of their interaction with white men takes place. Historically, white male/black female contact occurred under situations in which black women held roles of inferior status, e.g., housekeepers or maintenance staff. In contrast, black women now frequently interact with white men as equals in the workplace, if not in many instances as superiors. These more egalitarian interactions have a greater probability of resulting in the establishment of respect, friendship, and in some instances, romantic attraction.

• WHITE WOMEN ARE DRIVING HARDER ROMANTIC BARGAINS

Finally, white women today, like all women, are asking for more fairness in their romantic relationships. This fact probably has increased the white man's willingness to explore new romantic markets in search of better deals. In short, white women may appear comparatively less attractive as romantic partners, and at the same time black women are becoming ever more attractive as romantic partners.

Dating White—Should You?

By dating white, you are likely to increase your pool of romantic eligibles, and hence your probability of finding a romantic partner. I have tried not to say whether you should or should not date white. Ultimately, you must make your own decision anyway. I have merely attempted to provide some insight into this debate, which is so often full of heat and so seldom offers any light. As you know, there are strong social sanctions against black-white romance. Those who elect to go against the social norm should assess their degree of personal security, as they will at times meet tremendous opposition from both blacks and whites.

15 Odds To A Good End: A Review

ONE OF MY MAJOR ASSUMPTIONS throughout this book has been that you will have a better romantic life if you have a solid understanding of both why and how romantic relationships work as they do. Some chapters focused on why things work as they do, while others offered specific advice as to what you might do if and when you are confronted with a given romantic opportunity or situation. Furthermore, much of what has been discussed is pertinent to all romantic relationships, but the bulk has focused on getting new relationships off the ground.

We have covered considerable territory. We have looked at some of the reasons why you may be inclined to date whom you do, the implications of skin color and beauty, and productive things to do between romantic relationships. We spent a number of pages discussing the need to understand and assess your Romantic Market Value (RMV). We focused on the importance of placing yourself in the right place—which is always in the way of romance—and of doing so at the right time. Distinctions were made between "like," love, and lust, and some suggestions were made to show you how to tell the difference between these three emotions.

Our discussion of sex considered the potential implications of when, where, and with whom. Creating the perception of fairness in relationships was pointed out as a key to promoting romantic satisfaction. We considered the different sources of power in romantic relationships and how certain styles of wielding power have the potential either to enhance or to harm your relationship. And we discussed why some blacks date white, and how a positive outlook is likely to bring about positive romantic outcomes.

It is my hope that you found the many points made in this book to be pertinent to your own romantic situation. I believe that practicing even a few of these suggestions will substantially increase your probabilities of finding and sustaining romance.

A few additional observations, some old, some new, are worth emphasizing. A few of them come to mind as a consequence of comments and suggestions from colleagues, friends, critics, and even some strangers. These are the final thoughts I want you to consider.

Be Realistic

The black romantic market is a tough place. These are difficult times for black people in general, not just for black singles. The changing expectations in the behavior of men and women, in addition to the fact that black men in particular have been losing economic and educational ground since the mid-seventies, have made establishing romantic relationships more difficult than ever.

Black singles *should not blame each other* for this situation. Instead, I suggest that you be realistic in your romantic aspirations. Don't make a difficult search even more so by carrying around an inflated notion of your own romantic desirability. As my teen-aged nephew used to say, "Be for real." In addition, give both yourself and your potential partners a break: don't expect to receive more from your partner than you have to offer him or her. Such behavior is a sure cause of disappointment.

Be Positive

Don't let the demographics of the black romantic marketplace, the horror stories of others, or your own past unpleasant experiences get you down. Instead, start each new relationship thinking about what you want to happen *now*, rather than what happened in the past. I cannot emphasize enough how important it is to be positive in both your attitude and behavior. You *can* create positive self-fulfilling prophecies. You must be upbeat. Let your positive attitude show—send flowers and silly notes, offer assistance when possible, and, if you are inclined to do so, bake your partner a pie (it worked for my friend James).

Be Your Best—Immediately

If there is someone who interests you, attempt to present yourself to this person in a positive manner as quickly as you can. Not only am I suggesting that you make a good first impression, but I am suggesting that you do it sooner rather than later. By hesitating to put your best foot forward quickly, you may lose out on a romantic opportunity. Don't think that your virtues will become apparent to someone with the passage of time. They may, but by then the potential partner may have already become involved with someone else—and both of you may be sorry you were such slow starters.

Get Out There

Consistently put yourself in the way of romance. You must be seen to be "chosen." Your ideal romantic partner is unlikely to walk into your living room on a Saturday night and block your view of the television. You have to play to win, and in this case you have to increase your probabilities of winning by increasing the number of opportunities you have to play.

Remember, it's all about probabilities. Get out there—go to that art show, house party, or jazz concert. If you have a friend to go out with, fine; if not, that's fine, too. It's O.K. to go to functions alone. After all, if you stay at home, you'll stay alone, too. Besides, an unaccompanied man or woman is seen as being more approachable; and let's face it, being approached is what you're trying to make happen.

Be Fair

As a black person, your partner, like yourself, is likely to face unfair situations almost daily. Who needs more of the same in their romantic lives? Consequently, I urge you to create fairness in your relationships; share in the costs of romance, not just the benefits. Don't hide behind outdated ideas of how men and women are supposed to behave. Help with washing the dishes; contribute to the cost of the movie. You and your date are more likely to stay in a relationship if you feel you get as much out of it as you put in.

Be Productive Between Relationships

Get in the habit of using time between romantic partners to your advantage. The bottom line is always to attempt to enhance your romantic desirability between relationships. This is the best time to improve or increase your romantic assets—such as your looks, interpersonal skills, and material and intangible assets. This way you are in a better position for your next relationship, because you will have improved your RMV and have more to offer that next partner.

Date People Who Like You

Attempt to select partners whom you feel genuinely like you. Those romantic candidates who like you are your best romantic bets. Dating someone who likes you increases the probabilities that you will be treated well. There is something alluring about trying to *make* someone like or love us, but it rarely works. The reverse of this suggestion is also true: attempt to date someone you genuinely like, rather than someone who merely meets your objective criteria in a partner.

Date People Who Are (Already) Happy

Seek out romantic partners who seem to have good temperaments. In other words, date people who are generally in a good mood. Some people are frequently mad or irritated about something: their jobs, the weather, the traffic, their families, even you. They are often quick to show anger. None of us is able to keep someone like this happy all the time. If your romantic partners are inclined to be unhappy, you're not likely to change that, and then you too are likely to become unhappy.

Give Your Partners Space

Don't crowd your date. It is often suggested that black men are especially fearful of entrapment, but black women are, too. Provide your date with room in the relationship. Give him or her the chance to phone you back, or choose a social activity, or simply go home. Be prepared to spend time away from your partner—every moment doesn't have to be spent together. No one is responsible for your total entertainment. People rebel against partners who try to consume all of their time. You are apt to find that it isn't so much that they want to do things without you, but rather they want to feel they have the option to do so.

Don't Become A Romance Junkie

Meeting and dating new people can be exciting, and perhaps addictive. Indeed, the early phases of romance are likely to be among the most exciting times in the course of your dating activities. It is easy to see how some people fall in love with falling in love. Because of the higher ratio of eligible black females to males, the tendency to become a romance junky probably occurs more frequently among black men than women. But it is a risk for anyone who has had a variety of romantic partners.

Continuing to seek out new and exciting relationships may retard the development of your long-term relationships, because you may be forever looking to re-create a certain romantic high that is felt only at the onset of romance. Unfortunately, it never seems to last, and you may be inclined to think, "Well, maybe the next time." Don't bet on it! Attempt instead to seek enjoyment in other aspects of romance, such as deeper intimacy and the sharing of common experiences and friends.

Be Tolerant

One day during the final stages of writing this book, I found myself in a checkout line at a grocery store. Behind me was a rather stout, elderly, black man, whom I imagine must have been in his late sixties. Having become obsessed with finding out everything I could to make this book complete, I asked him if he had a wife. He proudly said yes. In fact, he said, he'd been married for over forty years. I quickly asked him, "What's your secret?" In a rather soft-spoken tone, he told me, "There ain't no secret—sometimes we get along and sometimes we don't, but we keep on going." I was blown away by the brilliant simplicity of his answer.

For those of you who live life in the fast lane, this illustration may offer important insight. It is obvious that many black singles have come to expect their romantic encounters to be instant winners. If things don't go right immediately, they are inclined to scream, "Next!"

Thus the wisdom of the old man's observation may be on target. It suggests that you should not expect your relationship to be great all the time—it won't be. Instead you must try harder to accommodate yourself to the not-so-great times. View these times as part of the romantic process, rather than as products of unpardonable character flaws in your partner or yourself.

In closing, let me point out that nobody is successful all the time. This is so regardless of how high your RMV is, or how physically attractive you might be. So don't give up if you get turned down. Just grab the rebound and try again. In your search for romance, being rebuffed provides you with two choices: either try this same person again, or move on to someone else. But you should never assume that your situation is hopeless and abandon your search for a suitable partner. This is a hard fact to remember, and something I have had to remind myself of on quite a few occasions. However, it should now be clear to you that you possess everything you need in order to enhance your romantic life. All you need to do is to use those insights, resources, and skills currently at your disposal—and do so earnestly and deliberately. Keep in mind that all you need to find in order to experience a better romantic life is just *one* romantic partner who suits you. Remember—stay upbeat and keep a positive attitude.

Selected Readings

For those readers wishing to obtain additional information on factors affecting romantic relationships, the following list of selected readings should prove helpful.

Romantic Attraction

Duck, S. (1986) *Human Relationships: An Introduction to Social Psychology.* Sage Publications.
Hendrick, S. and Hendrick, C. (1992). *Liking, Loving and Relating.* Brooks/Cole.

The Dynamics of Color and Beauty

Boyd-Franklin, N. (1989). Racism, racial identification, and skin color issues. In *Black Families in Therapy.* Guilford Press.
Cross, W. (1991). *Shades of Black: Diversity in African American Identity.* Temple University Press.
Hatfield, E. and Sprecher, S. (1986). *Mirror Mirror: The Importance of Looks in Everyday Life.* State University of New York Press.
Russell, K.; Wilson M. and Hall, R. (1992). *The Color Complex: The Politics of Skin Color Among African Americans.* Harcourt Brace.

Power and Communication

Peplau, L. (3rd Ed.)(1984). Power in dating relationships. In J. Freeman (Ed.), *Women: A Feminist Perspective.* Mayfield.
Tannen, D. (1991). *You Just Don't Understand.* Ballantine.

Economic and Political Factors

Farley, R. and Allen, W. (1989). *The Color Line and the Quality of Life in America.* Oxford University Press
Madhubuti, H. (1991). *Black Men: Obsolete, Single, Dangerous?* Third World Press
Wilson, W.J. (1987). *The Truly Disadvantaged.* University of Chicago Press

Selected Readings

Social and Psychological Factors

Guttentag, M. and Secord, P. (1983). *Too Many Women? The Sex Ratio Question.* Sage Publications.

Jackson, J. (Ed.) (1991). *Life in Black America.* Sage Publications.

Staples, R. and Johnson, L. (1993) *Black Families at the Crossroads: Challenges and Prospects.* Jossey-Bass.

Staples, R. (1981). *The World of Black Singles.* Greenwood Press.

References

These works served as resource materials during the writing of this book.

Adams, G. (1977). Physical attractiveness research: toward a developmental social psychology of beauty. *Human Development,* 20, 217-239.

Adams, J. (1965). Inequity in social exchange. In L. Berkowitz (Ed.), *Advances in Experimental Social Psychology.* New York: Academic Press, 267-297.

Altman, I. and Taylor, D. (1973). *Social Penetration: The Development of Interpersonal Relationships.* New York: Holt, Rinehart, and Winston.

Amodeo, J. and Amodeo, K. (1986). *Being Intimate: A Guide to Successful Relationships.* New York: Arkana.

Andersen, S. and Bem, S. (1981). Sex typing and androgyny in dyadic interaction: individual differences in responsiveness to physical attractiveness. *Journal of Personality and Social Psychology,* 41(1), 74-86.

Archer, R. and Burleson, J. (1980). The effects of timing of self-disclosure in attraction and reciprocity. *Journal of Personality and Social Psychology,* 38, 120-130.

Argyle, M. and Dean, J. (1965). Eye contact, distance and affiliation. *Sociometry,* 28, 289-304.

Argyle, M. and Furnham, A. (1983). Sources of satisfaction and conflict in long-term relationships. *Journal of Marriage and the Family,* 45(3), 481-493.

Aronson, E. and Linder, D. (1965). Gain and loss of esteem as determinants of interpersonal attractiveness. *Journal of Experimental Social Psychological,* 1, 156-171.

Aronson, E.; Willerman, B. and Floyd, J. (1966). The effect of a pratfall in increasing interpersonal attractiveness. *Psychonomic* Science, 4, 227-228.

Ashmore, R. and Del Boca, F. (Eds.) (1986). *The Social Psychology of Female-Male Relations: A Critical Analysis of Central Concepts.* Orlando, FL: Academic Press.

Atkinson, M. and Gan, B. (1985). Marital age heterogamy and homogamy. *Journal of Marriage and the Family,* 47(3), 685-691.

Backman, C. and Secord, P. (1959). The effect of perceived liking in interpersonal attraction. *Human Relations,* 12, 379-384.

Bahn, S.; Chappell, C. and Leigh, G. (1983). Age at marriage, role enactment, role consensus, and marital satisfaction. *Journal of Marriage and the Family,* 45(4), 795-803.

References

Bales, R. (1970). *Personality and Interpersonal Behavior.* New York: Holt, Rinehart, and Winston.

Ball, R. and Robbins, L. (1986). Black husbands' satisfaction with their family life. *Journal of Marriage and the Family,* 48, 849-855.

Bell, R.; Daly, J. and Gonzalez, M. (1987). Affinity-maintenance in marriage and its relationship to women's marital satisfaction. *Journal of Marriage and the Family,* 49(2), 445-454.

Bell, R. (1963). *Marriage and Family Interaction.* Homewood, IL: The Dorsey Press, Inc.

Berg, J. and McQuinn, R. (1986). Attraction and exchange in continuing and non-continuing dating relationships. *Journal of Personality and Social Psychology,* 50(5), 942-952.

Berg, J. (1984). Development of friendship between roommates. *Journal of Personality and Social Psychology,* 46(2), 346-356.

Bernhard, K. (1986). *Jealousy: Its Nature and Treatment.* Springfield, IL: Charles C. Thomas.

Berscheid, E.; Dion, K.; Walster, E. and Walster, G. (1971). Physical attractiveness and dating choice: A test of the matching hypothesis. *Journal of Experimental Social Psychology,* 1, 173-189.

Berscheid, E. (1986). On understanding emotion. *Journal of Social and Personal Relationships,* 3(4), 515-517.

Blumberg, R. and Roye, W. (1979). *Interracial Bonds.* New York: General Hall, Inc.

Booth, A. and Hess, E. (1974). Cross-sex friendship. *Journal of Marriage and the Family,* 36, 38-47.

Booth, A. and Edwards, J. (1985). Age at marriage and marital instability. *Journal of Marriage and the Family,* 47(1), 67-75.

Booth, A.; Brinkerkoff, D. and White, L. (1984). The impact of parental divorce on courtship. *Journal of Marriage and the Family,* 46(1), 85-94.

Bowen, G. and Orthner, D. (1983). Sex-role congruency and marital quality. *Journal of Marriage and the Family,* 45(1), 223-230.

Brockner, J. and Swap, W. (1976). Effects of repeated exposure and attitudinal similarity on self-disclosure and interpersonal attraction. *Journal of Personality and Social Psychology,* 33, 531-540.

Brown, D. and Gary, L. (1985). Social support network differentials among married and nonmarried black females. *Psychology of Women Quarterly,* 9(2), 229-241.

Buss, D. (1984). Toward a psychology of person-environment (PE) correlation: the role of spouse selection. *Journal of Personality and Social Psychology,* 47(2), 361-377.

Byrne, D.; Clore, G., Jr. and Worchel, P. (1966). Effect of economic similarity-dissimilarity on interpersonal attraction. *Journal of Personality and Social Psychology,* 4, 220-224.

Cash, T. and Derlega, V. (1978). The matching hypothesis: physical attractiveness among same-sexed friends. *Personality and Social Psychology Bulletin,* 4, 240-243.

Cate, R.; Lloyd, S.; Hentin, J. and Larson, J. (1982). Fairness and reward level as predictors of relationship satisfaction. *Social Psychology Quarterly,* 45(3), 177-181.

Cazenave, N. (1983). Black male-female relationships: the perceptions of 155 middle-class men. *Family Relations*, 32, 341-350.

Centers for Disease Control. (1991). *HIV/AIDS Surveillance Report*. Atlanta: Centers for Disease Control.

Chaiken, S. (1979). Communicating physical attractiveness and persuasion. *Journal of Personality and Social Psychology*, 37, 1387-1397.

Chapman, A. (1986). *Man Sharing: Dilemma or Choice*. New York: William Morrow & Co.

Cherlin, A. (1981). *Marriage, Divorce, Remarriage*. Cambridge, MA: Harvard University Press.

Clark, K. and Clark, M. (1947). Racial identification and preference in Negro children. In T.M. Newcomb and R.J. Hantley (Eds.), *Readings in Social Psychology*. New York: Holt, Rinehart and Winston. 169-178

Clark, M. and Mills, J. (1979). Interpersonal attraction in exchange and communal relationships. *Journal of Personality and Social Psychology*, 37, 17-24.

Cretser, G. and Leon, J. (Eds.) (1982). *Intermarriage in the United States*. New York: The Haworth Press.

Davis, J. (1976). Self-disclosure in an acquaintance exercise: responsibility for level of intimacy. *Journal of Personality and Social Psychology*, 33, 787-792.

Davis, J. (1978). When boy meets girl: sex roles and the negotiation of intimacy in an acquaintance exercise. *Journal of Personality and Social Psychology*, 36, 684-692.

Davis, L. and Proctor, E. (1989). *Race, Gender and Class: Guidelines for Practice with Individuals, Families and Groups*. Englewood Cliffs, NJ: Prentice Hall.

Davis, L. and Strube, M. (1993). An assessment of romantic commitment among black and white dating couples. *Journal of Applied Social Psychology*, 23 (3), 212-225.

Davis-Brown, K.; Salamon, S. and Surra, C. (1987). Economic and social factors in mate selection: an ethnographic analysis of an agricultural community. *Journal of Marriage and the Family*, 49(1), 41-55.

De Turck, M. and Miller, G. (1986). The effects of husbands' and wives' social cognition on their marital adjustment, conjugal power, and self-esteem. *Journal of Marriage and the Family*, 48, 715-724.

DeMaris, A. and Leslie, G. (1984). Cohabitation with the future spouse: its influence upon marital satisfaction and communication. *Journal of Marriage and the Family*, 46(1), 77-84.

Derlega, V.; Wilson, M. and Chaikin, A. (1976). Friendship and disclosure reciprocity. *Journal of Personality and Social Psychology*, 34, 578-582.

Dermer, M. and Pyszczynski, T. (1978). Effects of erotica upon men's loving and liking responses for women they love. *Journal of Personality and Social Psychology*, 36, 1302-1309.

Dermer, M. and Thiel, D. (1975). When beauty may fail. *Journal of Personality and Social Psychology*, 31, 1168-1176.

Dewsbury, D. (1981). Effects of novelty on copulatory behavior: the Coolidge effect and related phenomena. *Psychological Bulletin*, 89, 464-482.

Dion, K.; Berscheid, E. and Walster, E. (1972). What is beautiful is good. *Journal of Personality and Social Psychology*, 24, 285-290.

References

Dion, K. and Dion, K. (1975). Self-esteem and romantic love. *Journal of Personality*, 43, 39-57.

Dion, K. (1987). Integrating social psychology and the psychology of gender. *Contemporary Psychology*, 32(1), 35-37.

Fairchild, H. (1985). Black singles: gender differences in mate preferences and heterosexual attitudes. *The Western Journal of Black Studies*, 9, 69-73.

Falbo, T. and Peplau, L. (1980). Power strategies in intimate relationships. *Journal of Personality and Social Psychology*, 38, 618-628.

Folkes, V. and Sears, D. (1977). Does everybody like a liker? *Journal of Experimental Social Psychology*, 13, 505-519.

Fossett, M. and Kizcolt, K. (1993). Mate availability and family structure among African-Americans in U.S. metropolitan areas. *Journal of Marriage and the Family*, 55, 288-302.

Franck, K. (1980). Friends and strangers: the social experience of living in urban and non-urban settings. *Journal of Social Issues*, 36(3), 52-71.

Gaelick, L.; Bodenhausen, G. and Wyer, R., Jr. (1985). Emotional communication in close relationships. *Journal of Personality and Social Psychology*, 49(5), 1246-1265.

Gary, L. (1986). Predicting interpersonal conflict between men and women. *American Behavioral Scientist*, 29, 635-646.

Gary, L. (Ed.) (1981) *Black Men*. Beverly Hills, CA: Sage Publications.

Gary, L. and Leashore, B. (1982). The high risk status of black men. *Social Work*, 27, 54-58.

Glick, P. (1985). Orientations toward relationships—choosing a situation in which to begin a relationship. *Journal of Experimental Social Psychology*, 21 (6), 544-562.

Glick, P. and Spanier, G. (1980). Married and unmarried cohabitation in the United States. *Journal of Marriage and the Family*, 42, 19-30.

Glick, P. and Lin, S. (1986). Recent changes in divorce and remarriage. *Journal of Marriage and the Family*, 48, 737-747.

Goldman, W. and Lewis, P. (1977). Beautiful is good: evidence that the physically attractive are more socially skillful. *Journal of Experimental Social Psychology*, 13, 125-130.

Gonzales, M.; Davis, U.; Loney, G.; Lukens, C. and Junghans, C. (1983). Interactional approach to interpersonal attraction. *Journal of Personality and Social Psychology*, 44(6), 1192-1197.

Gottman, J.; Notarius, C.; Markman, H.; Bank, S. and Yoppy, B. (1976). Behavior exchange theory and marital decision making. *Journal of Personality and Social Psychology*, 34, 14-23.

Gray-Little, B. (1982). Marital quality and power processes among black couples. *Journal of Marriage and the Family*, 44(3), 633-646.

Gray-Little, B. and Burks, N. (1983). Power and satisfaction in marriage: a review and critique. *Psychological Bulletin*, 93(3), 513-538.

Greer, G. (1984). The uses of chastity and other paths to sexual pleasures. *Ms.*, 12(10), 53, 58, 60, 96.

Hammond, J. and Enoch, J. (1976). Conjugal power relationships among black working class families. *Journal of Black Studies*, 1, 107-128.

Hariton, B. and Singer, J. (1974). Women's fantasies during sexual intercourse. *Journal of Consulting and Clinical Psychology*, 42, 313-322.

Hartup, W. and Rubin, Z.(Ed.) (1986). *Relationships and Development*. Hillsdale, NJ: Lawrence Erlbaum Associates.

Hatfield, E. (1984). The dangers of intimacy. In V.J. Derlega (Ed.), *Communication, Intimacy, and Close Relationships*. New York: Academic Press, 207-220.

Hatfield, E. and Walster, W. (1985). *A New Look at Love*. New York: University Press of America.

Hazan, C. and Shaver, P. (1987). Romantic love conceptualized as an attachment process. *Journal of Personality and Social Psychology*, 52(3), 511-524.

Hendrick, C. and Brown, S. (1971). Introversion, extroversion, and interpersonal attraction. *Journal of Personality and Social Psychology*, 20, 31-36.

Hendrick, C. and Page, H. (1970). Self-esteem, attitude similarity, and attraction. *Journal of Personality*, 38, 588-601.

Hendrick, C. and Hendrick, S. (1983). *Liking, Loving, and Relating*. Belmont, CA: Wadsworth, Inc.

Hendrick, L. and Hendrick, S. (1986). A theory and method of love. *Journal of Personality and Social Psychology*, 50, 392-402.

Hill, C.; Rubin, Z. and Peplau, L. (1976). Breakups before marriage: The end of 103 affairs. *Journal of Social Issues*, 32(1), 147-168.

Hill, C.; Rubin, Z.; Peplau, L. and Willare, S. (1979). The volunteer couple: sex difference, couple commitment, and participation in research in interpersonal relationships. *Social Psychology Quarterly*, 42, 415-420.

Honeycutt, J.; Wilson, C. and Parker, C. (1982). Effects of sex and degrees of happiness on perceived styles of communicating in and out of the marital relationship. *Journal of Marriage and the Family*, 44(2), 395-406.

Howard, J.; Blumstein, P. and Schwartz, P. (1986). Sex, power, and influence tactics in intimate relationships. *Journal of Personality and Social Psychology*, 51(1), 102-109.

"J". (1969). *The Sensuous Woman*. New York: Lyle Stuart.

Jackson, J. (1975). The attitudes of black females toward upper and lower class males. *Journal of Black Studies*, 1, 107-128.

Jackson, J. (1978). But where are all the men? In R. Staples (Ed.), *The Black Family: Essays and Studies*. Belmont, California: Wadsworth, pp. 110-117.

Jacob, A. and Williams, J. (1985). Effects of premarital sexual standards and behavior in dating and marriage desirability. *Journal of Marriage and the Family*, 47(4), 1059-1065.

Jedlicka, D. (1984). Indirect parental influence on mate choice: a test of the psychoanalytic theory. *Journal of Marriage and the Family*, 46(1), 65-70.

Kallen, D. and Doughty, A. (1984). The relationship of weight, the self-perception of weight, and self-esteem with courtship behavior. In *Obesity and the Family*. New York: Haworth Press, Inc., 93-114.

Kelley, H., et al. (1983). *Close Relationships*. New York: W.H. Freeman.

Kenrick, D. and Cialdini, R. (1977). Romantic attraction: misattribution versus reinforcement explanations. *Journal of Personality and Social Psychology*, 35, 381-391.

Kenrick, D. and Johnson, G. (1979). Interpersonal attraction in aversive environments: a problem for the classical conditioning paradigm? *Journal of Personality and Social Psychology*, 37, 572-579.

Kersten, L. and Kersten, K. (1981). *The Love Exchange*. New York: Fredrick Fell.

Kinnaird, K. and Gerrard, M. (1986). Premarital sex behavior and attitudes toward marriage and divorce among young women as a function of their mother's marital status. *Journal of Marriage and the Family*, 48, 757-765.

Kline, A. and Meley, M. (1973). *Dating and Marriage: An Interactionist Perspective*. Boston: Holbrook Press, Inc.

Krebs, D. and Adinolfi, A. (1975). Physical attractiveness, social relations, and personality style. *Journal of Personality and Social Psychology*, 31, 245-253.

Lavin, T., III (1987). Divergence and convergence in the causal attributions of married couples. *Journal of Marriage and the Family*, 49(1), 71-80.

Lawrence, L. (1982). *Couple Constancy: Conversations with Today's Happily Married People*. Ann Arbor, MI: UMI Research Press.

Lee, J. (1973). *The Colors of Love: An Exploration of the Ways of Loving*. Don Mills, Ontario: New Press, (Popular Edition, 1976).

Lerner, H. (1986). *The Dance of Anger: A Woman's Guide to Changing the Patterns of Intimate Relationships*. New York: Harper and Row.

Levenson, R. and Gottman, J. (1983). Marital interaction: physiological linkage and affective exchange. *Journal of Personality and Social Psychology*, 45(3), 587-597.

Levine, S. (1987). More on the nature of sexual desire. *Journal of Sex and Marital Therapy*, 13(1), 35-44.

Levinger, G. and Ienn, D. (1967). Disclosure of feelings in marriage. *Merrill-Palmen Quarterly*, 13, 237-249.

Lewin, M. (1985). Unwanted intercourse: the difficulty of saying no. *Psychology of Women Quarterly*, 9(2), 184-192.

Lloyd, S.; Cate, R. and Hentan, J. (1984). Predicting premarital relationship stability: a methodological refinement. *Journal of Marriage and the Family*, 46(1), 71-76.

Malone, T. (1987). *The Art of Intimacy*. New York: Prentice Hall Press.

Maneker, J. and Rankin, R. (1985). Education, age at marriage and marital duration: is there a relationship? *Journal of Marriage and the Family*, 47(3), 675-683.

Margolin, L. and White, L. (1987). The continuing role of physical attractiveness in marriage. *Journal of Marriage and the Family*, 49(1), 21-27.

Mark, E. and Alpen, T. (1985). Women, men, and intimacy motivation. *Psychology of Women Quarterly*, 9(1), 81-88.

McAdoo, H. (1978). Factors related to stability in upwardly mobile black families. *Journal of Marriage and the Family*, 40, 761-776.

McAdoo, H. (Ed.) (1988). *Black Families*. Beverly Hills, CA: Sage Publications.

McCormick, N. (1979). Come-ons and put-offs: unmarried students' strategies for having and avoiding sexual intercourse. *Psychology of Women Quarterly*, 4, 194-211.

Mettee, D. and Wilkins, P. (1972). When similarity "hurts": the effects of perceived ability and humorous blunder upon interpersonal attractiveness. *Journal of Personality and Social Psychology*, 22, 246-258.

Michener, H.; Lawler, E. and Bacarack, S. (1973). Perception of power in conflict situations. *Journal of Personality and Social Psychology*, 28, 155-162.

Moschetta, E. and Moschetta, P. (1984). *Caring Couples: Inside the Vital-Total Relationship*. Farmingdale, NY: Coleman Publishing.

Murstein, B. (1972). Physical attraction and marital choice. *Journal of Personality and Social Psychology*, 22, 8-12.

Murstein, B. (1980). Mate selection in the 1970s. *Journal of Marriage and the Family*, 42, 777-792.

Murstein, B. (1970). Stimulus—value—role: a theory of marital choice. *Journal of Social Issues*, 32(1), 147-168.

Murstein, B. (1986). *Paths to Marriage*. Beverly Hills, CA: Sage Publications.

Nortin, A. and Moorman, J. (1987). Current trends in marriage and divorce among American women. *Journal of Marriage and the Family*, 49(1), 3-14.

O'Leary, V.; Unger, R. and Wallston, S. (1985). *Women, Gender, and Social Psychology*. Hillsdale, NJ: Lawrence Erlbaum Associates.

Parham, T. and Williams, P. (1993). The relationship of demographic and background factors to racial identity attitudes. *Journal of Black Psychology* , 19, (1), 7-24.

Peplau, L.; Rubin, Z. and Hill, C. (1977). Sexual intimacy in dating relationships. *Journal of Social Issues*, 33(2), 86-109.

Perlman, D. and Duck, S. (1987). *Intimate Relationships: Development, Dynamics, Deterioration*. Beverly Hills, CA: Sage Publications.

Reis, H.; Nezlek, J. and Wheeler, L. (1980). Physical attractiveness in social interaction. *Journal of Personality and Social Psychology*, 38, 604-617.

Reis, H.; Wheeler, L.; Spiegel, N.; Kernis, M.; Nezlek, J. and Perri, M. (1982). Physical attractiveness in social interaction: II. Why does appearance affect social experience? *Journal of Personality and Social Psychology*, 43(5), 979-996.

Ridley, C. and Avery, A. (1979). Social network influence on the dyadic relationship. In R.L. Burgess and T.L. Huston (Eds.), *Social Exchange in Developing Relationships*. New York: Academic Press.

Risman, B.; Hill, C.; Rubin, Z. and Peplau, L. (1981). Living together in college: implications for courtship. *Journal of Marriage and the Family*, 43, 77-83.

Rodgers, R. and Conrad, L. (1986). Courtship for remarriage: influences on family reorganization after divorce. *Journal of Marriage and the Family*, 48, 767-775.

Rogler, L. and Procidano, M. (1986). The effect of social networks on marital roles: a test of the Bott hypothesis in an intergenerational context. *Journal of Marriage and the Family*, 48, 693-701.

Rosenberger, L. and Strube, M. (1986). The influence of type A and B behavior patterns on the perceived quality of dating relationships. *Journal of Applied Social Psychology*, 16(4), 277-286.

Rubin, Z. (1970). Measurement of romantic love. *Journal of Personality and Social Psychology* 16, 265-273.

Rubin, Z. (1976). Naturalistic studies of self-disclosure. *Personality and Social Psychology Bulletin*, 2, 260-263.

Rubin, Z. and Levinger, G. (1974). Theory and data badly mated: a critique of Murstein's SVR and Lewis' PDF models of mate selection. *Journal of Marriage and the Family*, 36 (2), 226-231.

Rubin, Z.; Hill, C.; Peplau, L. and Dunkel-Schetter, C. (1980). Self-disclosure in dating couples: sex roles and the ethic of openness. *Journal of Marriage and the Family*, 42(2), 305-318.

References

Rubin, Z.; Peplau, L. and Hill, C. (1981). Loving and leaving: sex differences in romantic attachments. *Sex Roles,* 7, 821-835.

Rusbult, C. (1983). A longitudinal test of the investment model: the development (and deterioration) of satisfaction and commitment in heterosexual involvements. *Journal of Personality and Social Psychology,* 45(1), 101-117.

Rusbult, C.; Johnson, D. and Morrow, G. (1986). Impact of couple patterns of problem solving in distress and nondistress in dating relationships. *Journal of Personality and Social Psychology,* 50(4), 744-753.

Rusbult, C.; Johnson, D. and Morrow, G.D. (1986). Predicting satisfaction and commitment in adult romantic involvements: an assessment of the generalizability of the investment model. *Social Psychology Quarterly,* 49(1), 81-89.

Sabatelli, R. and Cecil-Pigo, E. (1985). Relational interdependence and commitment in marriage. *Journal of Marriage and the Family,* 47(4), 931-937.

Saegert, S.; Swap, W. and Zajonc, R. (1973). Exposure, context, and interpersonal attraction. *Journal of Personality and Social Psychology,* 25, 234-242.

Safilios-Rothschild, C. (1970). The study of family power structure: a review of 1960-1969. *Journal of Marriage and the Family,* 32, 539-552.

Safilios-Rothschild, C. (1976). A macro- and micro-examination of family power and love: an exchange model. *Journal of Marriage and the Family,* 38, 355-362.

Sanday, P. (1981). Female power and male dominance in the origins of sexual inequality. *Sex Roles,* 8, 1157-60.

Schumm, W. and Bugaighis, M. (1986). Marital quality over the marital career: alternative explanations. *Journal of Marriage and the Family,* 48, 165-168.

Schwartz, G., et al. (1980). *Love and Commitment.* Beverly Hills, CA: Sage Publications.

Seligman, C.; Fazio, R. and Zanna, M. (1980). Effects of salience of extrinsic rewards on liking and loving. *Journal of Personality and Social Psychology,* 38, 453-460.

Seyfried, B. and Hendrick, C. (1973). When do opposites attract? When they are opposite in sex and sex-role attitudes. *Journal of Personality and Social Psychology,* 25, 15-20.

Shaffer, D. and Ogden, J. (1986). On sex differences in self-disclosure during the acquaintance process: the role of anticipated future interaction. *Journal of Personality and Social Psychology,* 51(1), 92-101.

Sigall, H. and Landy, D. (1973). Radiating beauty: effects of having a physically attractive partner on person perception. *Journal of Personality and Social Psychology,* 28, 218-224.

Simpson, J.; Campbell, B. and Berscheid, E. (1986). The association between romantic love and marriage. *Personality and Social Psychology Bulletin,* 12(3), 363-372.

Snyder, D. and Smith, G. (1986). Classification of marital relationships. *Journal of Marriage and the Family,* 48, 137-146.

Snyder, M. and Cantor, N. (1980). Thinking about ourselves and others: self-monitoring and social knowledge. *Journal of Personality and Social Psychology,* 39, 222-234.

Snyder, M. and Simpson, J. (1984). Self-monitoring and dating relationships. *Journal of Personality and Social Psychology,* 47(6), 1281-1291.

Solomon, S. and Saxe, L. (1977). What is intelligent, as well as attractive, is good. *Personality and Social Psychology Bulletin*, 3, 670-673.

South, S. (1993). Racial and ethnic differences in the desire to marry. *Journal of Marriage and the Family*, 55, 357-370.

Spanier, G. (1976). Measuring dyadic adjustment: new scales for assessing the quality of marriage and similar dyads. *Journal of Marriage and the Family*, 38, 15-25.

Spanier, G. (1986). Citation classic—measuring dyadic adjustment—new scales for assessing the quality of marriage and similar dyads. *Current Contents/Social and Behavioral Sciences*, 51, 24.

Spence, J. and Helmreich, R. (1980). Masculine instrumentality and feminine expressiveness: their relationships with sex role attitudes and behaviors. *Psychology of Women Quarterly*, 5, 147-163.

Staples, R. (1979). Beyond the black family: the trend toward singlehood. *Western Journal of Black Studies*, 3, 150-157.

Stapleton, R.; Nacci, P. and Tedeschi, J. (1973). Interpersonal attraction and the reciprocation of benefits. *Journal of Personality and Social Psychology*, 28, 199-205.

Sternberg, R. (1986). A triangular theory of love. *Psychological Review*, 93, 119-135.

Sternberg, R. and Grajek, S. (1984). The nature of love. *Journal of Personality and Social Psychology*, 47(2), 312-329.

Stewart, A. and Rubin, Z. (1974). The power motive in the dating couple. *Journal of Personality and Social Psychology*, 34, 305-309.

Sullaway, M. and Christensen, A. (1983). Assessment of dysfunctional interaction patterns in couples. *Journal of Marriage and the Family*, 45(3), 653-660.

Surra, C. (1985). Courtship types: variations in interdependence between partners and social networks. *Journal of Personality and Social Psychology*, 49(5), 1246-1265.

Taylor, D. and Belgrave, F. (1986). The effects of perceived intimacy and valence on self-disclosure reciprocity. *Personality and Social Psychology*, 12(2), 247-255.

Taylor, R.; De Soto, C. and Lieb, R. (1979). Sharing secrets: disclosure and discretion in dyads and triads. *Journal of Personality and Social Psychology*, 37, 1196-1203.

Taylor, R.; Chatters, L.; Tucker, M. and Lewis, E. (1990). Developments in research on black families: a decade in review. *Journal of Marriage and the Family*, 52, 101-111.

Tedeschi, J. (1974). Attributions, liking and power. In T.L. Huston (Ed.), *Foundations of Interpersonal Attraction*. New York: Academic Press.

Thompson, M. (1981). Sex differences: differential access to poor sex role socialization? *Sex Roles*, 7, 413-424.

Thornton, B. (1977). Toward a linear prediction model of marital happiness. *Personality and Social Psychology Bulletin*, 3, 674-676.

Tolstedt, B. and Stokes, J. (1984). Self disclosure, intimacy and the depenetration process. *Journal of Personality and Social Psychology*, 46(1), 84-90.

Tyler, T. and Sears, D. (1977). Coming to like obnoxious people when we must live with them. *Journal of Personality and Social Psychology*, 35, 200-211.

U.S. Bureau of the Census (111th ed.)(1991). *Statistical Abstract of the United States*. Washington, D.C.: U.S. Government Printing Office.

References

Vaughan, D. (1986). *Uncoupling: Turning points in Intimate Relationships*. New York: Oxford University Press.

Vera, H.; Berardo, D. and Berardo, F. (1985). Age heterogamy in marriage. *Journal of Marriage and the Family*, 47(3), 553-566.

Waller, W. (1938). *The Family: A Dynamic Interpretation*. New York: Dryden. 162.

Walster, E. (1965). The effect of self-esteem on romantic liking. *Journal of Experimental Social Psychology*, 1, 184-197.

Warkeit, G.; Holzer, C.; Bell, R. and Arey, S. (1976). Sex, marital status, and mental health: a reappraisal. *Social Forces*, 55(2), 459-470.

Weitzman, L. (1985). *The Divorce Revolution: The Unexpected Social and Economic Consequences for Women and Children in America*. New York: The Free Press.

Werner, C. and Parmelee, P. (1979). Similarity of activity preferences among friends: those who play together stay together. *Social Psychology Quarterly*, 42, 62-66.

White, L. (1979). Erotica and aggression: the influence of sexual arousal, positive effect and negative effect on aggressive behavior. *Journal of Personality and Social Psychology*, 37, 591-601.

Wokel, S. (1973). Campus mate selection preferences—a cross-national comparison. *Social Forces*, 51, 471-476.

Wood, W. and Karten, S. (1986). Sex differences in interaction style as a product of perceived sex differences in competence. *Journal of Personality and Social Psychology*, 50(2), 341-347.

Zanna, M. and Pack, S. (1975). On the self-fulfilling nature of apparent sex differences in behavior. *Journal of Experimental Social Psychology*, 11, 583-591.

Zollar, A. and Williams, J. (1987). The contribution of marriage to the life satisfaction of black adults. *Journal of Marriage and the Family*, 49(1), 87-92.